URBAN
PUBLIC
FINANCE
IN CANADA

URBAN PUBLIC FINANCE IN CANADA

Richard M. Bird and N. Enid Slack

Butterworths
Toronto

Urban Public Finance in Canada
© 1983—Butterworth & Co. (Canada) Ltd.

Printed and bound in Canada
5 4 3 2 1   3 4 5 6 7 8 9/8

Canadian Cataloguing in Publication Data

Bird, Richard M., 1938–
   Urban public finance in Canada

Bibliography: p.
Includes index.
ISBN 0-409-81310-9

1. Municipal finance — Canada. I. Slack, N. E. (Naomi Enid), 1951–   II. Title.

HJ9350.B57   352.1'0971   C82-094778-4

The Butterworth Group of Companies

Canada:
Butterworth & Co. (Canada) Ltd., Toronto and Vancouver

United Kingdom:
Butterworth & Co. (Publishers) Ltd., London

Australia:
Butterworths Pty. Ltd., Sydney

New Zealand:
Butterworths of New Zealand Ltd., Wellington

South Africa:
Butterworth & Co. (South Africa) Ltd., Durban

United States:
Butterworth (Publishers) Inc., Boston
Butterworth (Legal Publishers) Inc., Seattle
Mason Publishing Company, St. Paul

Contents

Tables

Figures

About the Authors

Richard Bird is a professor of economics at the University of Toronto. He holds a doctorate from Columbia University and is the author of several monographs. He was an advisor to the Ministry of Finance for the government of Colombia and is a consultant to numerous foreign countries and international organizations. In addition to writing over 100 papers on public finance and economic development, Dr. Bird is a member of various professional associations in public finance and economics.

Enid Slack is an economic consultant specializing in public policy research. She also teaches part time at the University of Toronto. After completing her Ph.D. in Economics at the University of Toronto, Dr. Slack was a research officer at the Ontario Economic Council, specializing in public finance and urban affairs. She has written extensively on property taxes, intergovernmental transfers, and other aspects of urban public finance.

1 Introduction

The image of Canadians as inhabitants of a vast, almost primitive land has long had a strong hold not only on Hollywood filmmakers but also on Canadians themselves. In their innermost hearts many Canadians probably view themselves as representing "humanity" in the ongoing struggle between humanity and nature, particularly in the depth of winter or while fighting off insects during the annual summer foray into the primeval wilderness. In reality, however, Canada is one of the most urbanized countries in the world. Moreover, it is becoming more so every year. A growing number of Canadians live not only in cities but in large cities. As Table 1-1 shows, over three-quarters of the population of Canada now lives in urban areas, over 55 percent in urban areas with over 100,000 inhabitants, and almost 30 percent in the three largest urban areas — Toronto, Montreal, and Vancouver — alone. Although the rates of growth of cities of different sizes and in different parts of the country have changed markedly from time to time, the general move towards urban areas has been virtually unchecked over the more than a century of Canada's existence.

Canada today is thus a land of cities. The mythical "average" Canadian is not a farmer or a woodsman but an employee in an office or factory, who works and resides in or near a large city. Even those who do not live or work in such cities are almost always within their orbits of influence. How cities are governed and financed is therefore a matter of direct and immediate concern to all Canadians.

The main purpose of this book is to introduce to readers both some of the major issues in Canadian urban public finance and the potential contribution of economic analysis to resolving these issues. While the intended audience consists primarily of college and university students with little background in economics, it is hoped that the book will also be useful to others interested in urban affairs.

The book is organized as follows. Chapter 2 provides an overview of the context within which the urban public finance system in Canada functions. Questions such as the following are raised, and answered, in this chapter: How many local governments are there, what are the different types of local governments, and what do they do? Are there significant variations from province to province? How are urban capital expenditures financed and controlled? What is the role of provincial governments in local decision making? Perhaps the most important conclusion emerging from this discussion is the dominant role of the provinces in shaping Canadian

TABLE 1-1

The Urbanization of Canada, 1976

Province	Urban Population as Percent of Total	Percentage Increase in Urban Proportion Since 1951 %	Proportion in Urban Areas Over 100,000 %	Proportion in Urban Areas Over 1,000,000 %
Canada	75.5	20.0	55.7	29.5
British Columbia	76.9	8.6	59.6	50.2
Alberta	75.0	56.2	59.4	—
Saskatchewan	55.5	82.6	28.8	—
Manitoba	69.9	23.5	54.6	—
Ontario	81.2	10.6	63.0	34.0
Quebec	79.1	18.0	55.3	43.7
New Brunswick	52.3	22.8	16.9	—
Nova Scotia	55.8	0.9	31.5	—
Prince Edward Island	37.1	47.8	—	—
Newfoundland	58.9	37.9	25.9	—

SOURCE: Calculated from census data in Statistics Canada, *Perspectives Canada III* (Ottawa: Minister of Supply and Services, 1980), pp. 10, 192.

NOTE: "Urban" as defined in census; by "urban areas" is meant Census Metropolitan Areas, of which there are 23 in Canada.

urban public finance — a theme that runs throughout the book. The chapter concludes with a brief discussion of what many see as the major problem facing Canada's cities today. That is, "fiscal imbalance," or the apparent tendency, especially in these inflationary times, of expenditure needs to outrun revenue possibilities.

Chapter 3 turns from reality to review the theoretical literature on the urban public sector. Why do we have city governments anyway? What *should* the functions of such governments be? Should existing urban governments be expanded to encompass a greater area (amalgamation), or should they be collapsed into larger, regional governments? What does theory have to tell us about the "best" design of urban governments and finances? The chapter concludes with a brief look at an alternative approach to these questions that goes some distance to explaining the apparently tenuous connection between what economic theory suggests and what political reality produces.

Against the general empirical and conceptual background set out in chapters 2 and 3, the next four chapters consider several important questions in urban public finance. Chapter 4 first looks more carefully at what city governments actually spend their money on. Some evidence suggesting that many urban public services are becoming relatively more and more expensive to provide is then reviewed, and the chapter concludes with a discussion of some ways in which the efficiency with which cities function may be improved — a topic carried further in chapter 6. Complex issues such as productivity in the urban public sector and the role of budgeting and financial management are touched on in this discussion, though not developed at great length.

Chapter 5 begins with a brief overview of urban revenues, noting in particular the changing roles over time of property taxes, user charges, and provincial grants. The mainstay of present-day urban revenue structures, the property tax, is then discussed in some detail in the remainder of the chapter. Among the issues treated are the distributive effects of the property tax, its administration, the case for differentiating between land and buildings, and the case for differentiating between industrial and residential property.

Although there is much that is wrong with the present property tax system in many cities, there is also much that is right, and the general conclusion of this discussion is that no other general revenue source seems likely to supplant property taxes in Canadian local finance in the near future. Chapter 5 concludes with a discussion of other property-related revenues such as special assessments and a much briefer look at the possibility of financing Canadian cities through income and sales taxes.

Perhaps paradoxically, one way to alleviate some of the problems Canadian cities experience in financing adequate levels of services may be through more adequate and accurate pricing of many of those services. Chapter 6 is therefore devoted to a discussion of the revenue potential and economic advantages of such "user charges," and a brief examination of why they are in fact so little used in Canada. This chapter illustrates the considerable scope for pricing city services in such diverse cases as refuse collection and recreation. The chapter concludes with a consideration of the important and unique case of educational finance. The possible desirability of full provincial financing of such "soft" or "people-related" services as education is discussed in this section, which emphasizes another theme of this book, the inextricable entanglement of financial and structural issues.

Although the relative importance of provincial grants has declined slightly in recent years, such grants still constitute an extremely important part of the urban financial system. For this reason, chapter 7 is devoted to discussing the rationale for intergovernmental grants, the forms provincial-municipal grants take in Canada, and the probable effects of such grants on local expenditures and taxes. Perhaps the most important conclusion emerging from this discussion is to reinforce the earlier argument (see chapter 2) that cities are very much the creatures of the provinces; there is no such thing as "municipal home rule" in Canada. What city governments do, how they do it, and how they finance it are determined much more by provincial policies and actions than by any autonomous choices of city inhabitants.

Any reforms of urban finance thus imply corresponding reforms of provincial policies. This is perhaps one reason why it has as yet proven much harder to reform urban finance in Canada than to redraw urban boundaries. The latter can be done at provincial will, largely ignoring local wishes; the former, however, often would require provincial governments to intrude openly into the wallets of taxpayers, never a politically easy move. Nevertheless, the growing weight of urban representatives in provincial governments, like the growing weight of urban Canadians in the population as a whole, may in the future increase the sensitivity of provincial governments to urban needs and concerns. What form such a change might take — whether towards more or less municipal autonomy, for example — is not very clear, however, as is pointed out in the brief concluding chapter. And as this chapter suggests, it is seldom useful to consider problems of urban public finance in isolation from the more general problems of the public economy as a whole. The reverse is also true, however, in the sense that it is long past time for the needs for local services of the majority of Canadians who live in urban areas to be more explicitly taken into account at both the provincial and federal levels of government. Until an appropriate "urban partnership" can be developed to resolve these problems, it seems likely that Canadians and their cities will at best continue to "muddle through," though perhaps only with increasing difficulty as continual waves of technological and social change affect our lives and living patterns in ever more convoluted and complex ways.

No short review of the many, complex issues touched on in this book can be complete, of course. Much has necessarily been left out, and much else may be presented in a way that some may feel is too one-sided — though the only axe we are grinding is, for the most part, the economist's traditional one, namely, that economic efficiency matters with respect to urban public finance, as well as everywhere else. For those who want further details on the many subjects mentioned in this book, or alternative views, a fairly extensive list of references and sources has been included at the end of the book.

2 The Institutional Setting

Since cities are where most Canadians live, how well cities perform their functions and how those functions are financed constitute an important aspect of Canadian lifestyles. This chapter provides a brief overview of the institutional framework within which the urban fiscal system in Canada functions. It considers the structure of local governments, what municipalities do, the role of the provinces in shaping local decisions, particularly with respect to capital financing, and the extent of local "fiscal imbalance." The significant differences existing between provinces and between large and small municipalities are emphasized in chapters 4 and 5, where the pattern of urban expenditures and revenues is outlined in more detail. The most important conclusion emerging from this chapter is applicable across the country, however. It is that the provinces have such a high degree of control over local decisions that local governments of even the largest cities have relatively little flexibility with respect to either how they raise funds or how they spend them. It is therefore not possible to discuss urban public finance issues for long without broadening the discussion to the provincial and even federal sphere, for it is there that the crucial decisions determining local fiscal outcomes are necessarily made. This point is discussed further in chapter 8.

THE STRUCTURE OF LOCAL GOVERNMENT

At the beginning of the 1980s, there were over 4,000 local government units of various sorts in Canada, as shown in Table 2-1. Cities and towns exist in all provinces, and most also have villages, but in general the name, nature, degree of autonomy, and functions of these units vary widely from province to province, reflecting the diverse history of local government in different parts of the country.[1] Since each category means something different in each province, it is very difficult to compare the structure of local governments across the country. "Towns," for example, may have different statutory powers in different provinces. For this reason Table 2-1 does not provide nation-wide totals for each type of government unit.

Considerable variation in the structure of local governments is also suggested by the wide range in the total number of local units in each province, from 79 in Prince Edward Island to 1577 in Quebec. In recent years, there has been some trend towards larger local government units, with reforms of varying magnitudes in municipal organization being proposed in

TABLE 2-1

Local Governments in Canada, by Province

Province	Cities	Towns	Villages	Rural Municipalities	Townships	Other*	TOTAL
British Columbia	33	12	57	—	—	66	168
Alberta	12	110	163	—	—	80	365
Saskatchewan	11	137	347	299	—	—	794
Manitoba	5	35	40	105	—	17	202
Ontario	44	143	120	—	479	49	835
Quebec		272	270	—	153	882	1577
New Brunswick	6	21	88	—	—	232	347
Nova Scotia	3	39	25	24	—	—	91
Prince Edward Island	1	8	30	—	—	40	79
Newfoundland	2	166	—	—	—	147	315
							4773

SOURCES: Canadian Tax Foundation, *Provincial and Municipal Finances 1981*; *Almanac of Canada 1980, 1981*.

* "Other" includes a wide variety of other bodies: counties, municipal districts, improvement districts, drainage districts, townships, regional districts, special areas, local service districts, local government districts, metropolitan areas, communities, boroughs, community improvement committees, parishes, rural districts, united districts, districts and municipalities without designation.

at least seven provinces and carried out to some extent in five, particularly in New Brunswick and Ontario. In most instances, however, these reforms have resulted in the creation of new higher-level local government units rather than the suppression of existing units. The rationale of such reforms is discussed further in chapter 3.

ALLOCATION OF FUNCTIONS

The allocation of expenditure functions to municipalities also varies between provinces. As a rule the province provides services directly to unorganized areas, but the precise degree of direct provincial involvement in services to organized areas varies by province and by function. Expenditures that may appear to be "local" are in fact often controlled to a great extent by the province through such devices as grant programs, and the setting of standards; see chapter 7. Indeed, as discussed later in the present chapter, most provinces have established some type of municipal board or agency with quasi-judicial powers to oversee municipal activities, especially in the areas of land-use planning, capital expenditures, and borrowing.

Whatever the degree of provincial control may be, however, Canadian municipalities are involved to at least some extent in a variety of important expenditure responsibilities such as education, transportation, planning, protection to persons and property, health and social assistance, housing, industry and tourism, and recreation and culture.[2] Indeed, since local governments provide more "final" goods and services than any other level of government, the quantity and quality of local public-sector activity impacts more directly on the lives of Canadians than any other aspect of the public economy.[3] The condition of the streets they use, the safety of the homes they live in, the education of their children — these are the sorts of public-sector activities Canadians probably most care about, and they are, for the most part, the responsibility of local governments.

Local services are sometimes divided into two broad categories: "hard" services, or those whose benefits are related to property (and, as discussed in chapter 5, probably at least partly capitalized into the value of property), and "soft," or people-related services. The traditional municipal services of roads, sewers, fire protection, and so on fall for the most part into the first category, and such newer services as education, health, and social assistance into the second. Although this division is obviously to some extent arbitrary — recreation facilities, for example, provide services directly to people, but their proximity may raise property values, while police protect people as well as property — it has sometimes been suggested that the two types of services should be financed differently, with property-related activities being financed by property taxes and "people" services by more general, and probably provincial revenues. In part, this suggestion reflects the perception that the local fiscal "imbalance" of recent years (see later in this chapter) arises largely from the growing need to finance rapidly expanding "soft" services from the slowly growing traditional property tax base of local governments. In part, it reflects the view that the correct model for local government finance is the so-called "benefit" approach, under which, so to speak, property owners should pay only for what property owners get. For both these reasons, it has been argued, it is not right to expect local governments to finance "people" services, even if, for efficiency or other reasons, it is decided that they are to be the providers of such services. These points are discussed further in chapter 5.

Education through the secondary level is a local function in all provinces except New Brunswick, where it is a provincial responsibility, that is, it is the provincial government that collects the taxes, makes the expenditures, and determines the curriculum. Local school boards in New Brunswick play only a very minor, supplementary role. In all other provinces, primary and secondary education is formally a local responsibility, although as a rule the province maintains such control over funding, curriculum, and hiring that there is often very little flexibility left to the local school boards. In all cases, these boards are independent of municipal governments, although the municipalities are generally responsible for collecting school taxes levied on the municipal property tax base. In view of the unique importance and organization of the local education sector, education finance is discussed separately in chapter 6.

In the area of transportation, municipalities are generally responsible for local roads, with the province being responsible for intercity routes. Public transit is also a municipal responsibility, although it is financed, to varying degrees, by provincial subsidies. Some municipalities have a separate municipal transit authority, while others operate their transit systems through a city department.[4]

Planning initiatives are generally taken at the local level, but the province retains a significant advisory role over planning decisions, usually, as noted earlier, through a special supervisory body. Somewhat less provincial supervision occurs in British Columbia and Alberta.[5]

Other areas of local responsibility are police protection, fire protection, water, and sewage. Policing tends to be a local responsibility in organized areas and a provincial responsibility in unorganized areas. Although cities and towns usually have a municipal police force, some smaller municipalities contract with the RCMP or the provincial police force (in Ontario and Quebec) to provide police services. Fire protection is everywhere a local responsibility, with provinces sometimes providing some assistance. Water and sewage are also a local responsibility, sometimes provided by special public enterprises, but are generally funded, in part, by federal and provincial capital grants. As with respect to other urban services, the province often sets minimum standards for these services.

Responsibility for health and social assistance has largely been taken over by the federal and provincial governments. At most, municipalities may operate, but seldom pay for, hospitals and ambulance services. In larger cities they may perhaps also run a public health program. Although the municipal role in social assistance is also very limited, where there is joint federal-provincial-municipal funding under the Canada Assistance Plan (CAP), municipalities may pay as much as 25 percent of the cost of certain types of welfare, with 25 percent from the province and 50 percent from the federal government.

Finally, municipalities also play a limited role in terms of expenditures in the areas of housing, industry and tourism, and recreation and culture. Although some municipalities, usually only the largest, provide assisted housing and senior citizen housing, housing is largely a function of the federal government through CMHC and the various provincial housing ministries. Municipalities also operate cultural and recreational activities, usually of local interest, such as parks, libraries, and recreational centres. These too are often funded, in part, by provincial grants.

THE ROLE OF THE PROVINCE IN LOCAL DECISION-MAKING

Local governments in Canada are the creatures of the provinces. Since the British North America Act was first implemented, the provinces have had the exclusive right to create or disband municipal corporations. The provinces also determine the powers and responsibilities of their constituent municipalities, and hence their expenditure requirements. They also dictate which revenue sources are available to finance these expenditures. Municipalities can only undertake those functions assigned to them by the provinces.

In each province, there is generally a provincial statute governing various aspects of municipalities. Examples are The Municipal Act in Ontario, The Town Act in Prince Edward Island, and The Municipalities Act in New Brunswick. These Acts specify the functions municipal governments may undertake, the sources of revenue available to them, how and when budget decisions are made, the alteration of municipal boundaries, the composition of municipal councils, the passing of bylaws, and a number of other matters relating to the role of local governments in the several provinces. In most provinces, there are separate statutes for the larger municipalities — for example, each of the ten regional municipalities in Ontario plus Metropolitan Toronto has an additional, separate Act governing most of its functions. In addition, each province has a planning act that stipulates rules and regulations regarding municipal planning decisions, the development of regional and municipal plans, planning bylaws and sometimes provincial financial assistance for planning.[6]

Most provinces also have an assessment act that lays down rules for assessing real property for property taxes. In five of the ten provinces (Prince Edward Island, Nova Scotia, New Brunswick, Ontario, and British

Columbia) the assessment function is entirely a provincial responsibility. In the remaining provinces, although assessment is a municipal function, there is still some provincial role in assessing real property, whether it be the provision of manuals for assessors or provincial assessment of properties in all but the larger municipalities.[7]

Finally, there are various other provincial statutes that affect local government services — for example, The Clean Air, Water, and Soil Authority Act governing water and sewage works in municipalities in Newfoundland, or The Municipal Water Assistance Act in Saskatchewan, which specifies provincial-municipal grants for water and sewage and distribution facilities of local municipalities.

As described in the next section, most provinces have also established a board, commission, or quasi-judicial agency to oversee many of the functions of local governments — approval of capital expenditures, borrowing, planning decisions, and passing of municipal bylaws.

As is evident from this very brief description of how local governments fit into the provincial-municipal system, provincial intervention into local decisions is pervasive and takes many forms, from complete provincial control over certain functions to the specification of standards for local provision. Although there is variation from province to province, it is generally true that the province maintains at least some control over local borrowing, over the determination of the tax base for the major source of local revenues (the property tax), as well as the determination of property tax rates, over the restructuring of local government, over planning decisions, and over local expenditure patterns in general. In addition to the overall control of expenditures, the various provincial-municipal transfers, as shown in chapter 7, allow the province to maintain significant control of specific expenditure functions.

In reality, there is thus very little local autonomy for Canadian cities. The province determines the assessment base for the property tax and how much it will give out in provincial transfers on the revenue side, it determines which functions the municipalities can undertake on the expenditure side and then it requires municipalities to balance their budget on current account. With respect to capital expenditures, as shown in the next section, the province must generally approve all long-term borrowing. Local governments thus have little flexibility when it comes to local fiscal decisions — although the largest cities have a little more than other areas, largely because they are relatively less dependent on provincial grants (see chapter 5).

FINANCING CAPITAL EXPENDITURES

One area where all provinces exercise particularly tight control over local finance concerns capital expenditures and the issuance of debt. As a rule, the provinces both provide some sort of assistance for local capital borrow-ing and also require some form of provincial approval for long-term debt.

Debt finance by local governments is very different from debt finance by the federal government. To some extent at least, the federal government uses debt finance as a stabilization tool to achieve such economic goals as low unemployment, stable prices, and economic growth. Local govern-ments, on the other hand, do not have so clear a role to play in stabilization policy.[8] As discussed in chapter 3, the major task of a local government is to provide local public services to its residents, and the role of borrowing at the local level is usually to finance specific capital expenditures where the benefits are to be enjoyed by residents now and in the future. As mentioned earlier (see also chapter 5), the benefit principle of taxation that is fre-quently applied to local finance suggests that people should pay for public services in relation to the benefits they receive. To the extent, then, that the benefits from some projects are enjoyed in the future, it seems only fair that future residents should also share in the capital costs. In the pristine form of such "pay-as-you-use" financing, debt charges paid by each generation of future taxpayers would coincide with their use of the physical assets — roads, a recreation center, etcetera — built with the borrowed funds.[9]

Quite apart from the theoretical merits of borrowing for capital pro-jects, issuing bonds is often the only practical way to finance local capital expenditures, since it would be very difficult to use current revenues such as property taxes to make such large outlays in any given year. One capital project might account for a very large proportion of the budget in some municipalities for the year. By spreading the costs of a project over a period of time, there would be much less variation in tax rates on an annual basis. There appears, then, to be a strong case for financing capital projects at the local level through debt finance.[10]

Indeed, Canadian municipalities generally use debt finance to pay for that part of major capital works not financed through provincial grants.[11] In almost all cases, however, municipal governments are severely restricted by the provinces with respect to the amount of debt they can incur, the type of debentures they can issue, the length of term, the rate of interest, and the use of debt funds.

Some provinces require ministerial approval before debt can be in-curred, while others require municipalities to receive authorization from the relevant provincial agency (for example, the Municipal Capital Borrowing Board in New Brunswick, the Ontario Municipal Board, the Manitoba Municipal Board, the Local Government Board in Saskatchewan or the Local Authorities Board in Alberta). In some provinces, incurring debt also requires the approval of the electors. Three provinces (Nova Scotia, Mani-toba and, in some instances, Ontario) require municipalities to submit a five-year capital budget to the provincial minister or appropriate provincial agency. Some provinces have different restrictions for different types of municipalities. In Saskatchewan, for instance, the restrictions are more severe in terms of length of terms and size of loans, for rural municipalities than for urban municipalities. In British Columbia, the requirements are stricter for villages than for cities and towns, and in Prince Edward Island, only villages require the approval of the minister. With respect to debt finance, at least, the larger municipalities are treated somewhat differently.

Municipalities are also allowed to incur short-term debt on current account in order to meet expenditure requirements pending receipt of the current year's taxes. However, the amount of debt on current account is also severely restricted by the province. Usually, municipalities can go into debt up to some percentage of the previous year's tax levy, the precise percentage varying from province to province. Some provinces also require ministerial or board approval of short-term borrowing.

All provinces also provide some capital assistance to local governments. Some provinces (for example, Newfoundland, Nova Scotia, and New Brunswick) give grants to municipalities to pay principal and interest. Other provinces act as "lenders of last resort" — the province buys debentures that could not be sold elsewhere. The Newfoundland Municipal Financing Corporation, for example, sells provincially guaranteed debentures and uses the proceeds to purchase municipal debentures, thus lowering the interest rate for municipalities. The difficulties all but the largest cities have in borrowing on either national or international capital markets suggest that other provinces in the future might follow the path of the Municipal Finance Authority of British Columbia and the Municipal Finance Corporation of Nova Scotia, provincial bodies that in effect pool local borrowing needs and borrow on the security of the province as a whole.

This discussion of debt finance in Canadian municipalities provides still more evidence of the high degree of provincial control over local finances. Although the nature of control varies from province to province, no Canadian local government can incur any significant amount of long-term debt without the approval of the provincial government. An important advantage of this situation is that local governments in Canada, unlike local governments in the United States, are most unlikely to go bankrupt. But this result is achieved only at the expense of severe restrictions on local autonomy.

LOCAL FISCAL IMBALANCE

Surveys suggest that Canadians are sometimes so heavily influenced by their constant exposure to U.S. media that they tend to perceive American problems as existing in Canada, whether they do or not. In recent years, American discussion of local finance has been dominated by increasing reports of crisis: New York City's virtual bankruptcy in 1975; similar, if less acute, financial problems in Cleveland, Oakland, Detroit, etcetera — the litany of problems facing America's older cities seems as endless as the slums and decaying urban infrastructure that characterize so many of them. Faced with a continual need to raise local taxes to cope with expenditure pressures, local government officials have been squeezed in a fiscal vice both by their eroding tax bases and by the revolt of their remaining tax-payers as epitomized by California's famous "Proposition 13," which set a ceiling on property taxes in that state in 1978, and Boston's "Proposition 2-1/2" in 1980, which set an even more stringent limit. Fiscal crises and the imbalance between local revenues and expenditures are thus very real in the United States.

For the most part, however, these problems do not exist in Canada to nearly the same extent, nor, indeed, are they ever likely to emerge here with anything like the same force. This happy situation arises for many reasons. First, Canada's large cities are newer and, in large part, still growing, with the result that their fiscal base is not eroding.[12] Secondly, municipal govern-ments in Canada are not responsible for financing rapidly expanding "peo-ple" services to nearly the same extent as in some United States states; pro-vincial support of municipal finance and provincial assumption of local functions is much greater in Canada. Finally, provincial control of munici-pal finance is so tight that no Canadian city would ever be permitted to let its finances get as much out of control as those of New York and some other United States cities did.

Despite this relatively rosy picture, there has been continuing concern about the problem of local fiscal imbalance in Canada. Although the details of municipal expenditure patterns — including important differences be-tween provinces and by size of municipalities — are left for chapters 4 and 5, it may be useful to conclude this chapter by considering more closely the problem of local fiscal imbalance in Canada.

In simple terms, fiscal imbalance occurs when revenues fall short of ex-penditures. There are three relevant aspects of this imbalance that need to be discussed here: its measurement, its causes, and its significance.

At the local level, fiscal imbalance can be measured in two different ways — as expenditures less own-source revenues or alternatively, as ex-penditures less total revenues including intergovernmental transfers. Table 2-2 shows both measures of fiscal imbalance for local governments in Canada from 1967 to 1978.[13] The column headed "general expenditures less general revenues from own sources" shows the ability of local governments to meet expenditure requirements from their own revenue sources. On this measure, local fiscal imbalance has increased from $130 per capita in 1967 to $485 per capita in 1978, or from 45.3 to 52.2 percent of total expendi-tures. Transfers have also increased substantially over this period, however, so that the second measure of fiscal imbalance (expenditures less revenues) shows a much smaller increase over the period in per capita terms, from $25 in 1967 to $70 in 1978, and a *decline* in relative terms, from

8.8 to 7.5 percent of total expenditures. In other words, although the share of total current expenditures covered from local taxes and other "own-source" revenues declined slightly over this period, provincial grants increased sufficiently to more than compensate for this decline.

TABLE 2-2

Local Fiscal Imbalance, Canada, 1967-78

Year	General Expenditure Less General Revenues from Own Sources			General Expenditures Less General Revenues		
	$	Per Capita	As % Total Ex-penditure	$	Per Capita	As % Total Ex-penditure
1967	2,654,430	130	45.3	512,562	25	8.8
1968	3,012,413	146	45.9	588,694	28	9.0
1969	3,362,016	160	46.3	555,404	26	7.6
1970	3,760,751	177	46.8	476,184	22	5.9
1971	4,730,067	219	50.1	607,905	28	6.4
1972	5,141,855	236	50.1	689,052	32	6.7
1973	5,638,049	255	50.1	747,865	34	6.7
1974	6,970,174	311	52.4	1,019,588	45	7.7
1975	8,598,400	377	53.8	1,259,700	55	7.9
1976	9,653,502	420	52.2	1,452,275	63	7.9
1977[a]	10,048,043	432	51.0	1,274,046	55	6.5
1978[b]	11,396,374	485	52.2	1,635,726	70	7.5

SOURCE: Calculated from *Local Government Finance* (various years).

[a] Preliminary
[b] Estimates

Whatever its magnitude, fiscal imbalance at the local level occurs essentially because local revenue sources tend to grow more slowly over time than income, while local expenditures tend to grow more quickly.[14] Since local governments in Canada largely rely on property taxes for own-source revenues, their principal revenue source does not grow as automatically as do, say, income or sales taxes (see discussion in chapter 5). In order to raise more local taxes, constant reassessments, statutory changes in the tax base, or periodic changes in tax rates are required. A continuous imbalance between expenditures and revenues can in principle be rectified either by such changes on the revenue side or by a reduction in the rate of expenditure growth.

Is there local fiscal imbalance in Canada? Yes, if one considers own-source revenues; and no, if one considers all revenues. Whether there is imbalance or not, does it matter? It is clear, for example, that local revenues, notably the property tax, do not automatically expand as quickly as incomes in general; it takes a good deal of sweat, tears, and political blood to raise property taxes sufficiently to keep up with the pace of expenditure growth needed to maintain service levels (see chapter 4), and Canadian municipal politicians were no doubt grateful to be saved this effort by the expanding provincial grant finance of recent decades. It is by no means as clear they will be similarly spared in the 1980s, however, so we will no doubt hear renewed municipal pleas for access to such more painlessly expansible revenue sources as income and sales taxes in the future. The question, however, is whether municipal financial policy should be established to make life easier for politicians, or with other criteria in mind.

From another point of view, for example, a relatively inelastic revenue system may play an important and useful role in constraining the growth of the urban public sector.[15] When local officials and politicians want to increase expenditures, they can do so in these circumstances only by openly increasing taxes — and given people's apparently inherent dislike of paying taxes, one may therefore be much more certain that they get what they want than is likely to be true when an elastic tax system painlessly produces revenues that can be spent without overt public scrutiny and approval. Clearly, the view implicit in such statements of a modern, complete urban area as a sort of "town meeting" is highly idealized; nevertheless, as is suggested at the end of chapter 3, this "public choice" approach to questions of urban finance is a potentially powerful tool of analysis in approaching questions such as this. At the very least, it serves as a useful counterbalance to the usual equally implicit and idealized assumption in much discussion of the urban fiscal "problem," that benevolent public officials will use all the money that flows effortlessly into their hands, wisely.

The question of fiscal imbalance can be resolved in yet another way, probably more congruent with traditional Canadian attitudes, by stressing the need to match revenue-raising authority with expenditure responsibility if good fiscal decisions are to be made. From this point of view, there is indeed a problem revealed by the figures in Table 2-2 in that the responsibility of local authorities for the expenditures they make has been lessened by their increasing reliance on provincial transfers. Schemes such as those sometimes put forward to give local governments some unconditional access to provincial sales and income tax revenues would tend to exacerbate rather than relieve the problem, however, unless the municipalities are explicitly made responsible for levying their *own* taxes on these bases. A more acceptable solution viewed in this perspective would be to transfer responsibility for expenditures to the level of government that is providing the finance, namely, the province. This point is developed further with respect to education in chapter 6.

This section, and indeed this chapter, has introduced a number of important concepts — the "benefit" model, the "process" model, the central role of provincial governments in municipal finance, and so on — that are developed further in the context of urban public finance in Canada in chapters 4 through 8. Before proceeding along these lines, however, it will be both useful and salutary to consider more explicitly in the next chapter some of the theoretical analysis of the urban public economy that has emerged in recent years.

3 The Urban Public Economy

This chapter reviews the theoretical literature on the urban public economy, beginning with a brief consideration of the role of local governments within the context of a federal system. The first section introduces the concept of local public goods. The closely related concept of externalities is then discussed, followed by a brief consideration of income redistribution at the local level. A number of economic and political criteria determining the optimal structure of urban governments are then set out, followed by a review of several innovative types of government structures developed in Canada recently — metropolitan governments, regional governments, and various forms of annexation, consolidation, and two-tier levels of government. Finally, the last section of this chapter considers briefly what may be called a "political economy" perspective of the urban public economy, stressing the roles of various actors in the urban government game — politicians, bureaucrats, and citizens.

THE FUNCTIONS OF LOCAL GOVERNMENT

The role of local government must be considered in the broader context of the role of government in the economy. Three major functions of government are traditionally discussed in economics: the efficient allocation of resources, the redistribution of income, and the maintenance of stable employment, prices, and economic growth.[1] The appropriate division of these responsibilities between the various levels of government — federal, provincial, and local — is usually set out as follows.[2]

In the first place, because provincial and local economies are very closely linked, the use of monetary and fiscal policies by subnational governments to achieve the goals of stabilization policy (full employment, stable prices, and a reasonable level of economic growth) is not likely to be very efficient. Since capital and labor generally flow freely across governmental jurisdictions within a country, much of the impact of stabilization policies of one government unit will likely spill over into other jurisdictions.[3] Efficient stabilization policy by subnational governments, particularly local governments, is thus unlikely. Stabilization policy is thus definitely not an appropriate function for local government.[4]

Problems also arise if the distribution function is carried out by local governments. In particular, it is generally argued that redistribution should be carried out by higher levels of government because of the efficiency problems created by labor mobility at the local level. In other words, since people can easily move in response to the tax and transfer policies of local governments, attempts to redistribute income at this level of government can readily be offset. Largely for this reason, although the policies of local governments will of course affect the distribution of income, such redistribution should not be their major objective. Some aspects of redistribution at the local level are considered further later in this chapter.

In sharp contrast to stabilization and distribution, the allocation function *requires* a significant local government role if it is to be efficiently carried out. Some goods, called "public goods," have certain characteristics that make private provision very difficult. As is shown in the next section, for some of these public goods an optimal allocation of resources can be achieved only when such goods are provided by local government jurisdictions. Ideally, the jurisdictions that provide these goods and services should be defined to include all those people who demand the same public goods, and the benefits should be enjoyed by residents of those jurisdictions and not by anyone else. Unfortunately, as discussed below, jurisdictional boundaries do not always coincide with benefit boundaries, owing to spillovers. The optimal design of government units taking account of spillovers and other problems is a complex question that can be outlined only briefly in the present chapter. Nevertheless, it is clear that in terms of economic theory, the major role assigned to local governments is to provide certain governmental services whose benefits are spatially limited, thus aiding in the efficient allocation of resources between private and public sectors of the economy. Most of the remainder of this chapter therefore focusses on this allocative function of local governments.

LOCAL PUBLIC GOODS[5]

To understand the basic allocative function of local governments requires a brief background review of the basic "efficiency conditions" that ideally need to be satisfied with respect to any good or service. In particular, those who are familiar with elementary economics will recall that under certain conditions market competition will result in the most efficient allocation of resources, that is, in a situation in which reallocating resources will not make anyone better off without making someone else worse off.

Consider an economy with 2 persons (A and B), 2 goods (X and Y), and 2 factors of production (K and L). An efficient allocation of resources requires that three conditions be met:

1. $MRS_{X,Y}^{A} = MRS_{X,Y}^{B}$

The first efficiency condition requires that the marginal rate of substitution (MRS) between X and Y be the same for both individuals, A and B. In other words, the rate at which individual A substitutes X for Y, at the margin, is the same as the rate at which B substitutes X for Y at the margin. If this condition is not met, then individual A, for example, can be made better off by exchanging some X — which is, we assume, worth less to him at the margin than the Y he can get in exchange — for some Y with B, who is also better off because the additional Y is worth more to her than the X she gives up. As long as such "gains from trade" are possible, exchange will continue up to the point at which no exchange can make the two parties better off — at which point condition (1) is satisfied.

$$2. \quad MRTS_{K,\,L}^{X} = MRTS_{K,\,L}^{Y}$$

The second efficiency condition states that the marginal rate of technical substitution between the two factor inputs must be the same for both products X and Y. This means that the rate at which factor K is substituted for factor L in the production of X, at the margin, is the same as the rate at which K is substituted for L in the production of Y, at the margin. If these rates differ, more of both X and Y can be obtained by moving capital (K) and labor (L) from the production of one good to the other, and rational decision makers will continue to substitute one factor for the other up to the point at which no further gains in production can be realized by doing so, that is, until condition (2) is satisfied.

$$3. \quad MRS_{X,\,Y}^{A} = MRS_{X,\,Y}^{B} = MRT_{X,\,Y}$$

The final efficiency condition requires that the common marginal rate of substitution between the two goods A and B be equal to the marginal rate of transformation (MRT) between X and Y. In other words, the rate at which Y can be substituted for X is exactly the same in both production and consumption. On the production side, reallocating resources will not increase the output of one good without reducing the output of another, and on the consumption side, no exchange will make anyone better off without making someone else worse off. When the three efficiency conditions set out above are satisfied, the market will yield an efficient allocation of resources in the sense that no one can be made better off without making someone else worse off.

These conditions hold only in the market for *private* goods, however. *Public* (or social) goods, on the other hand, have two characteristics that result in market failure — nonrivalness in consumption and nonexcludability. "Nonrivalness in consumption" means that one person's consumption of the good or service does not affect the consumption of others. For example, if a public park exists, one person's enjoyment of it is not affected by other people enjoying it, at least up to the point of congestion. Once the good — the park — is provided, it is available to everyone, and each person's consumption of it is equal to the total amount available (X^A, or A's consumption of X, equals X^B, equals X). Nonrivalness in consumption occurs wherever the marginal social cost of providing a good to an additional person, once it is already being provided to one person, is zero. Since the efficient price to charge is equal to the marginal social cost, the resulting price is zero. Since obviously costs cannot be covered at a zero price, such goods must generally be provided by government.[6] Nonrivalness in consumption thus requires public provision.[7]

The second characteristic of a public good, "nonexcludability," means simply that it is very difficult, or very costly, to exclude anyone from enjoying the benefits of the public good, even if the good does not have the nonrivalness characteristic. For example, it may be possible to exclude people from using public roads, but it would be very costly, with present technology, to do so.

Local public goods, like public goods in general, possess the same two characteristics, but the benefits enjoyed are limited to those in a particular geographic area. In other words, local public goods are available to people residing in a particular jurisdiction. Adding a spatial dimension means that individuals in different jurisdictions may demand different quantities of public goods. Although very few urban public services are "pure" public goods, many urban services do exhibit some measure of each of these characteristics — parks, street lighting, and roads are examples[8] — and thus generally require some government intervention if the optimal amount of such services is to be provided.

The two characteristics of public goods noted above — nonrivalness in consumption and nonexcludability — alter the third efficiency condition for private goods set out earlier. This condition now becomes:

3a. $MRS_{X,Y}^{A} + MRS_{X,Y}^{B} = MRT_{X,Y}$

The efficient outcome now occurs where the *sum* of the marginal rates of substitution equals the marginal rate of transformation.

The reason for this change reflects the critical differences in the markets for private goods and public goods illustrated in Figures 3-1 and 3-2. In each Figure there are assumed to be two individuals, A and B, with demand curves D_A and D_B. Moreover, the distribution of income and the prices of all other goods are taken as given.

In the case of the private good, the total demand (D_{A+B}) is the horizontal summation of the individual demand curves for A and B. For example, in Figure 3-1, given the price P_O, individual A demands quantity Q_A and individual B demands Q_B. The total demand is Q_{A+B}.

Turning to the public good, it should first be noted that the individual demand curves are drawn on the assumption that individuals reveal their preferences for public goods. A quantity of the public good Q is provided to everyone, and each individual consumes the same amount, Q. The total demand curve D_{A+B} is then the _vertical_ summation of the individual demand curves for A and B. The amount that each individual is willing to pay for quantity Q reflects his valuation of the marginal unit. For example, in Figure 3-2, individual A will pay P_A and individual B will pay P_B. The total price paid for Q is thus P_{A+B}, the sum of the prices paid by each individual. Equilibrium occurs where demand equals supply at price P_{A+B} and quantity Q.

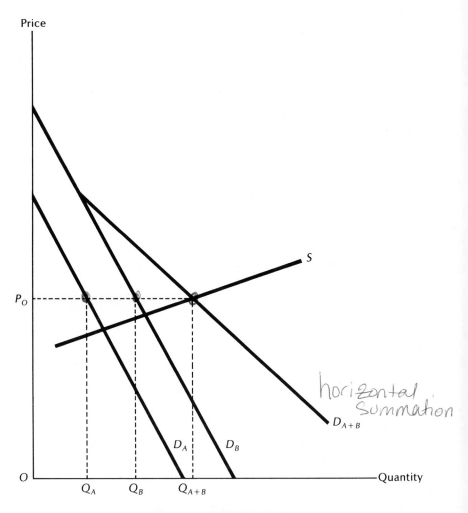

Figure 3-1   Private Good

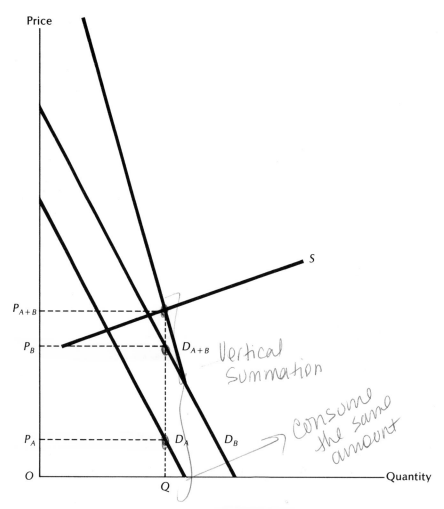

Figure 3-2   Public Good

The vertical distance under each individual demand curve reflects the marginal benefit derived by each individual from the consumption of the good. From Figure 3-1 it can be seen that, in equilibrium, the marginal benefit for each individual equals the marginal cost represented by the supply curve ($MB_A = MB_B = MC$) for the private good. From Figure 3-2, it can be seen that, in equilibrium, the marginal benefit for any given quantity of the public good supplied (for example, Q) is the vertical summation of each individual's marginal benefit, and the sum of the marginal benefits equals the marginal cost ($\Sigma MB = MC$).

In principle, the demand and supply of urban public goods can thus be considered in terms similar to any other goods. The quantity demanded —

measured, for example, in physical units, such as number of refuse containers collected per year — would show how much local residents demand at any given price. The quantity supplied, also measured in physical units, reflects the marginal cost per unit supplied. Urban governments would then presumably choose to produce that level of public services where demand just equals supply.

Unfortunately, choosing the appropriate level of output is not so simple. A first problem is to define and measure the output of urban public services. This is fairly easy for services such as refuse collection and water delivery but becomes much more difficult when considering services like education, police, and parks. What measures can be used to reflect the output of these services? Often proxies for output measures have to be used: number of students enrolled, expenditures on education, crime rate, and so forth.

Even if satisfactory output measures can be found, there is a second problem in trying to estimate demand. Because of the two basic characteristics of public goods — nonrivalness in consumption and nonexcludability — there is no mechanism by which consumers will voluntarily reveal their preferences for these goods. In the case of private goods, variations in price will cause consumers to reveal the quantity they demand of that good or service; as argued in chapter 6, many services commonly provided by urban governments can, in fact, be priced in this way. With pure public goods, however, the quantity cannot be varied because everyone enjoys the same amount. The result is that there is no incentive for consumers to reveal how much they will pay for it. Consumers will try to become "free riders" by understating the value of the good so that they will not have to pay much for it, in the belief that the good will be provided anyway. "Impure" public goods — combining characteristics of both public and private goods — will obviously fall in between these two extremes.

Without any reliable price signals, it is very difficult to estimate the demand for various public goods and services. For some urban public services, however, it is possible to determine consumer preferences because price signals are available. For example, since one can exclude people from making use of public utilities such as electricity and water service, it is possible to have consumers reveal preferences for these services. Similarly, services for which at least partial private market substitutes exist, such as education, and those that are reflected in differential property values may in effect be "priced" to some extent, as discussed in chapters 5 and 6.

This problem is not as serious a limitation on the usefulness of this analysis as may at first appear, however. In reality there are probably relatively few "pure" public goods at the local level. Often, for example, the benefits received from some good, such as a park or a fire station, "taper" with distance, that is, decline as one lives further away. In such cases, at least in part, "public" goods may be "priced" by being capitalized in residential land values (see also chapter 5). In other instances, local public services in effect have some characteristics of both private and public goods; that is, the direct benefit may be received by an identifiable, and excludable, individual but there are also indirect benefits received by others as a result of his or her direct consumption of the service. In this "spillover" case, as discussed later in this chapter, there may be some possibility of using a variant of the usual pricing mechanism to generate information on preferences. A third potential method of obtaining such information is known as the "Tiebout hypothesis," as discussed in the next section.

THE TIEBOUT HYPOTHESIS   *(VOTING for Public Goods)*

The "Tiebout hypothesis," first put forward by Tiebout (1956), states that if there are a large number of communities, each with a different tax and public-service package, and if consumers are perfectly mobile between jurisdictions, then an optimal allocation of public goods within communities will result. In effect, consumers reveal their preferences for local public goods by moving to the jurisdiction that has the tax and service package that most closely satisfies their preferences. The result of "voting with one's feet" in this way would be a large number of homogeneous communities with revenues and expenditures that reflect the preferences of their residents. In this sense, a marketlike solution, yielding an efficient allocation of resources, may exist for local public goods that does not exist for public goods at other levels of government. The Tiebout hypothesis is based on a number of assumptions of varying degrees of plausibility. Consumers are fully mobile and will move to that community whose tax-and-expenditure mix best suits their preferences; consumers know the tax-and-expenditure patterns of each community; there are many communities offering different mixes; restrictions due to employment opportunities are not considered; there are no externalities, positive or negative, between communities; for every pattern of community services, there is an optimal community size; and communities below the optimal size try to attract new residents to lower average costs, whereas communities above the optimal size try to decrease population. Some of these assumptions cast doubt on the meaningfulness of this approach.

For the Tiebout hypothesis to function properly, for example, consumers must be perfectly mobile. If consumers are dissatisfied with the tax-expenditure package provided in the jurisdiction in which they are residing, they will simply move to another jurisdiction. This assumption ignores the significant real and psychic costs involved in moving. Residents are in reality likely to try to change the tax-expenditure package through the political system, by registering their preferences in their voting patterns and in other ways, before moving from the jurisdiction. The Tiebout model ignores any form of political expression other than "voting with their feet." This point is discussed a little further in the final section of this chapter.

Another important shortcoming of the Tiebout model is that it assumes that there are no externalities in service provision. In fact, the likelihood of interjurisdictional spillovers (externalities) would be even greater where there are many small, homogeneous, local jurisdictions as there would be in a Tiebout world. This problem is discussed further in the next section.

Despite the important restrictions implicit in such assumptions, Tiebout's hypothesis is important because it shows that, under certain conditions, the optimal amount of local public goods will be provided by a system of local governments, in effect because consumers will reveal their preferences for *local* public goods. As noted above, consumers have no incentive to reveal their preferences for public goods in general because of the characteristic of nonexcludability. If an individual cannot be excluded from enjoying the benefits of a good, he has no incentive to state accurately his preference for it. A rational consumer will tend to understate his true preference and enjoy the service being provided without having to pay for it. Without knowledge of consumer preferences the government has no signals (such as price signals in the private market) as to how much service to provide. With local public goods, according to the Tiebout hypothesis, consumers reveal their preferences by voting with their feet.

Several empirical studies have been undertaken to test the Tiebout hypothesis (see Bird and Slack [1978a], Appendix A). It is generally argued in these studies that, to the extent that people are influenced by the taxes and expenditures of jurisdictions when choosing a place to live, relative property values should reflect this. For example, a community with relatively low taxes and high public expenditures will, other things being equal, attract more residents compared to other communities. The resulting increased demand for properties in that community will bid up property values. In equilibrium, property taxes and public expenditures will be capitalized, all or in part, into property values. Although the empirical evidence can best be characterized as mixed, the results of some of these studies generally suggest that taxes and public expenditures are capitalized at least partly into property values, thus lending some apparent support to the Tiebout hypothesis. Other studies suggest, on the contrary, that this test of Tiebout's hypothesis is backward (Edel and Sclar [1974], Hamilton [1976]) since land prices will, except for locational differences, be equal across jurisdictions, so that evidence of capitalization suggests that an efficient mix of public services is *not* being provided (that is, some properties are in effect earning scarcity rents because public services are over-supplied in the jurisdiction in which they are located).[9] Even if the empirical evidence on capitalization were clearer, then, the degree of support lent to the Tiebout hypothesis by such evidence is far from clear.

To summarize the argument to this point, in economic terms the major task of local government is to provide local public goods and services. Estimating the demand for local public goods and services is very difficult, however, both because the outputs cannot be easily defined and because there are no price signals to force consumers to reveal their preferences. The difficulties created by these problems can easily be exaggerated, however; various proxies can be used to measure output, many public services can be priced to at least some extent in various ways, and there may be something in the Tiebout hypothesis that people vote with their feet for local services. Moreover, as discussed later in this chapter, in at least an aggregative sense the political process can to some extent substitute for the market process as a way of revealing preferences.

EXTERNALITIES

As noted earlier, very few public services provided by urban governments are really "pure" public goods, but many do have characteristics that can lead to market failure and necessitate some form of government intervention to achieve efficient resource allocation. One such characteristic is an externality or spillover.[10] An externality occurs whenever the activity of one party affects the well-being of other parties, without being priced. Such an activity can result in external benefits or costs. An oft-cited example is education. When an individual receives an education there are obvious personal benefits. However, there are also at least some external benefits — it is usually assumed, for example, that society as a whole benefits from a more educated populace. The social benefits of education may thus exceed the private benefits to the individual. The individual has no incentive to increase these external benefits by getting more education than is in one's own interest, however.

Interjurisdictional spillovers occur when the expenditures and revenues of one particular government unit spill over into other government jurisdictions. For example, if one jurisdiction decides to clean up water pollution in a river located within its boundaries, municipalities downstream will also benefit from the expenditures on pollution control without having to pay for them.

The existence of such spillovers can lead to a misallocation of resources, with too many or too few goods being provided. In the case of an external economy, the party generating the spillover does not enjoy any of the external benefits and consequently has no incentive to take them into account in determining what level to supply. In equating *private* marginal benefits and *private* marginal costs, the individual will choose a level of output that is less than optimal from society's point of view. There will be an underallocation of resources to the activity generating the external benefit. Similarly, where there is an external diseconomy, the individual will not take account of the external costs imposed on others and will tend to over-allocate resources to the activity generating the external cost.

Some form of government intervention is therefore required to encourage the party generating the externality to equate marginal *social* benefits with marginal *social* costs. Consider the example in Figure 3-3 of external benefits. The private demand for the good is represented by D_P, which is the horizontal summation of all individual private demands for the good. The external benefits are reflected in D_X, which is a pseudodemand curve by those who enjoy these benefits. D_T is the vertical summation of individual demands. The total benefits derived from the good are shown by D_T, which is the vertical summation of D_P and D_X. The optimal output from society's point of view is Q_O, which takes account of private and external

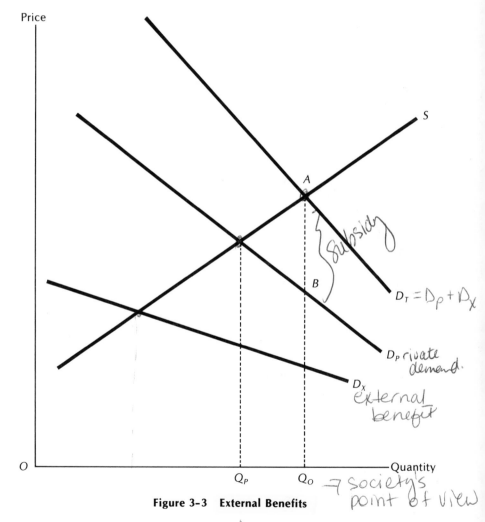

Figure 3-3   External Benefits

benefits. The market mechanism will result in an output of Q_P, which is less than optimal. A per unit subsidy of AB to the party generating the external benefit will result in the optimal output Q_O being reached.

Figure 3–4 shows the case of external costs. The market supply is represented by S_P, and S_X shows the external costs imposed on other parties. S_T reflects the total cost of supplying the particular good, and it is the vertical summation of the private costs S_P and external costs S_X. The optimal output is Q_O; the market mechanism will result in an output of Q_P, which is greater than the optimal. A per unit tax of AB on the party generating the external cost will result in the optimal output Q_O being produced.

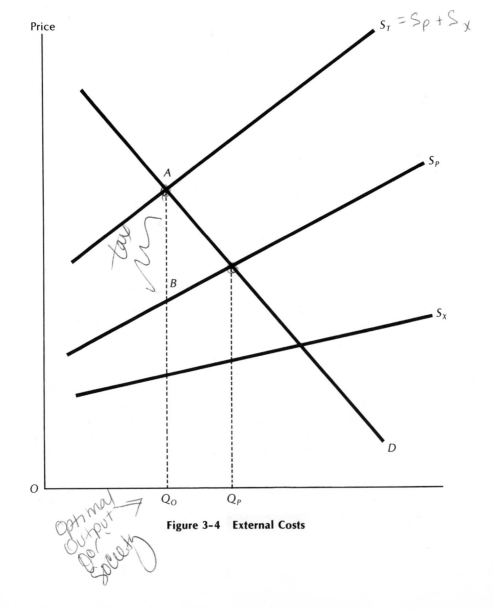

Figure 3–4   External Costs

The above analysis is difficult to apply, since the general lack of information on the relevant supply and demand curves means that in practice it is usually impossible to calculate the size of the taxes or subsidies needed to achieve optimality. Nevertheless, the idea of the divergence between social and private returns from particular activities is an important aid to understanding the rationale for many government activities in the real world.

Some form of government intervention is usually required to correct the market failure. There are three possibilities. The first is to subsidize the jurisdiction generating the externality so that it will consider the external benefits as well as the benefits to its own residents; the second is to internalize the externality by making the government jurisdiction large enough so that all of the benefits of the good are enjoyed within the jurisdiction; and the third is for the jurisdictions concerned to negotiate an appropriate arrangement directly. Subsidies intended to account for externalities are discussed further in chapter 7, while the relevance of the spillover criterion for designing governmental structure is discussed later in this chapter. The third approach — sometimes called the "Coase solution" — is only applicable in very limited circumstances.[11]

INCOME DIFFERENTIALS

An important factor affecting the allocation of resources to local public goods is the availability of resources. Although the demand for local services may be the same in two jurisdictions, the revenues available to meet these demands may differ. Thus, in order to provide the same level of services in two different jurisdictions, it may be necessary to levy different tax rates. A municipality relatively rich in terms of the size of its tax base will not have to levy as high a tax rate to provide a given level of services as would a relatively poor municipality. Private-sector resources will thus tend to flow to richer areas, where the fiscal differential (taxes related to expenditures) is more favorable.

The ability to levy taxes — the fiscal capacity of a jurisdiction — will thus affect the ability of different local governments to provide local goods and services. A municipality with a small tax base will tend to undersupply local public goods, whereas a municipality with a large tax base — particularly one where many taxes are in effect "exported" to nonresidents (see chapter 5) — will oversupply local goods. Two possible solutions to the resulting misallocation of resources are possible. The first is to subsidize the provision of public goods in the relatively poor jurisdictions with some form of equalization grant; this is discussed further in chapter 7. The second is to create larger and more heterogeneous units of government, thereby reducing the tax base differentials giving rise to the problem. This possible criterion for designing the size of local government units is discussed in the next section.

DESIGNING GOVERNMENTAL STRUCTURE AND FINANCE

The discussion thus far has concentrated mainly on the demand for local public goods. On the supply side, in addition to the problem of how much of the public good to supply, the spatial dimension of local public goods adds some additional complications.[12] For example, the precise location of the local public good has to be determined and the number of users has to be estimated. How large should schools, parks, or recreation facilities be? How far apart should they be located? How many of these services should be located within each jurisdiction? Is it better to have schools that are smaller but closer together? What are the tradeoffs in making such decisions? These and other issues must be taken into account in designing the structure and finance of local governments.

In principle, the main objective in designing the optimal government structure should be to maximize the welfare of individuals. The welfare of individuals is assumed to be determined, at least in part, by the satisfaction they receive from the local public goods and services provided. The optimal level of government then, is that the best provides the desired level of local public goods at the least cost. Within this general framework, several criteria may be used to design governmental structure: economies of scale, spillovers, redistribution, demand considerations, and political efficiency. The first three of these criteria on the whole suggest that a relatively large level of government is appropriate for the provision of local public services, while the last two tend to support smaller levels of government. In general, the tradeoffs between these criteria in choosing the optimal size of government suggest that the appropriate size will likely be different for different services.[13]

Economies of scale occur where the per unit cost of producing a particular service falls as the quantity of service provided increases. Where such economies exist a larger level of government could provide local public services more efficiently, or cheaply, because it can more easily reap economies of scale in production. The optimal size of government, from the point of view of economies of scale, would be the one that can achieve the lowest possible cost of production, and jurisdictions must be large enough to have a sufficient population to support this least-cost method of production.

There are several problems with this approach, two of which may be mentioned here. First, each urban service will likely achieve the lowest per unit cost at a different scale of production. The optimal size of government may be different for fire services than for education, for example. This leads to problems in determining the optimal-sized jurisdiction. One way to get around this problem may be to have a two-tier government (for example, a metropolitan or regional level of government) in which the upper tier provides those services for which there are significant economies of scale and the lower tier provides the remaining services.

The second problem arises because the jurisdiction that provides the service is not necessarily the one that consumes it. If consumers are located in adjacent jurisdictions, then the producing jurisdiction could sell output to them. The producing jurisdiction could benefit from economies of scale in production without having to be part of a larger jurisdiction, that is, without requiring the large population to be located within its own boundaries. In other words, economies of scale can be reaped even in a fragmented system; a larger jurisdiction is not necessarily required to achieve economies of scale because the demand and supply of local government services can be separated.

Some empirical work has been done to estimate the extent to which there are in fact economies of scale in urban public services. For example, Hirsch (1959) estimated cost functions for police services, fire services, refuse collection, water, sewage, and education. His results showed that expenditures per capita declined with the quantity provided for water and sewage services, but not for any of the other urban services examined. Hirsch concluded that, since water and sewage represent only eight to ten percent of total municipal expenditures for most cities in the United States, the consolidation of jurisdictions could not really be justified on efficiency grounds. He also found that for some services, expenditures per capita actually rose as output expanded, indicating that there were diseconomies of scale. A number of subsequent studies have also attempted to estimate cost functions for various urban public services. These studies found some economies of scale for water, sewers, and transportation, but not for police, refuse collection, recreation, or planning.[14] However, even if larger government units could more easily reap economies of scale in the provision of some of the "hard" services, such as water, sewers, and transportation, there are, as noted above, other ways to reap economies of scale in service provision besides having large jurisdictions.

Spillovers constitute a second argument in favor of relatively large local government units. As pointed out earlier, when some of the benefits from a particular local good may spill over into other jurisdictions, an underallocation of resources to that good is likely to result. Moreover, since the jurisdictions into which the benefit spills are paying nothing for it, they may choose to provide more of the service in total for their citizens than they otherwise would.

One way to remove the inefficiency in resource allocation resulting from spillovers is to design government jurisdictions large enough so that all of the benefits from a particular public service are enjoyed within that jurisdiction.[15] Such boundary readjustments could in principle internalize the externality. Here again there are at least three problems, however. Not only may there be no natural division into jurisdictions, but also the optimal-sized jurisdiction will likely be different for different services, and in addition the optimal jurisdiction from the point of view of internalizing externalities may conflict with the optimal size required to reap economies of scale.

Distributive arguments are at least as important as efficiency arguments in designing governmental structure. As noted earlier, general economic reasoning suggests that distributional goals will be more efficiently achieved by fairly large, heterogeneous government jurisdictions.[16] In an area that is divided into relatively small, homogeneous units — along Tiebout lines, for example — there are likely to be some rich communities and some poor communities. In such circumstances, although the rich communities will have a more than adequate tax base with which to provide services, the demands for some services, such as education and welfare, may not be particularly large. The poor communities, on the other hand, may want far more services but will only have a small tax base on which to levy taxes. An obvious possible solution to this problem is to consolidate the two areas into one jurisdiction, in effect taxing the rich municipalities and using some of the proceeds to subsidize the poor municipalities. Of course, it may be very difficult to get the rich communities to go along with such a consolidation. An alternative approach is to shift the redistributive function to a higher level of government. For example, in most parts of Canada, welfare is administered largely by the provincial and federal levels of government, leaving only a residual role for the municipalities.

Demand considerations are just as important as supply considerations in determining the optimal size of local governments. The Tiebout hypothesis outlined earlier suggested, for example, that people "vote with their feet," moving to the jurisdiction with the tax-expenditure package that most closely resembles what they desire. This model requires, among other things, a large number of homogeneous communities, each with a different tax and expenditure package, in order to permit consumers to reveal their preferences and thereby achieve an optimal allocation of public goods. The Tiebout approach thus lends support to the notion that a system of smaller, more homogeneous local governments may be more efficient than one consisting of fewer, larger, and more heterogeneous units. A large, diversified urban area, for example, will be less efficient in meeting the demands of residents because it tends to provide a uniform level of public services to people who have diverse preferences for such services.

Political criteria as well as such economic criteria must also be taken into account in designing optimal governmental structure. One such criterion is "access," by which is meant the desirability of the government unit being small enough for the average citizen to have some influence on local decisions that affect him or her.[17] Because local citizens have access to the government in this sense, it is argued that their interests will be reflected to at least some extent in government decisions. Government units should therefore be designed to allow for as much citizen participation as is feasible without sacrificing performance of functions. This "access" criterion thus suggests that smaller government jurisdictions are more efficient politically.

This political case for decentralization is simply a pragmatic recognition of the fact that groups caught by the chance of history within the same national boundaries differ in relevant ways, and in the absence of good reason to the contrary they should presumably be free to exercise these differences. In this sense, local autonomy minimizes political externalities due to heterogeneity (preference revelation costs), though perhaps at the expense of increasing decision-making costs. It also leads to more responsiveness to real citizen needs.

Other possible political criteria include geographic area sufficiency and legal and administrative ability.[18] "Geographic area sufficiency" means that the geographic area covered for the provision of services should be large enough to allow for "effective" performance. This criterion is obviously rather similar to the economies of scale argument. The jurisdiction has to be sufficiently large to make the expenditure on particular services worthwhile. Alternatively, small jurisdictions could perhaps buy the service from another municipality.

Legal and administrative ability requires the jurisdiction to have the appropriate legislation to govern service provision,[19] adequate personnel to operate the various service functions, and adequate resources with which to finance them. A larger, richer municipality will tend to attract more specialized and more highly paid personnel and will also have a larger tax base, though not necessarily larger intergovernmental transfers, on which to draw. This too is an aspect of economies of scale.

Other possible political criteria include the need for specialized knowledge of local conditions; the desirability of flexibility and trial by experiment with respect to changes in governmental functions; and the desirability of promoting local initiative and responsibility. Obviously this list is neither complete nor mutually exclusive, nor are any of these criteria particularly clear.

Even the brief discussion in this section should have made it clear that there is no simple answer to the question, "What is the optimal government structure?" The answer really depends on the criteria to be satisfied. For example, on the assumption that the consumption of most collective services is spatially differentiated, and that people have different tastes for collective services, collective demands will in general be most efficiently satisfied by a high degree of autonomous fiscal decentralization. Similarly, if one is interested in fostering citizen participation in local political decisions or access to local government, smaller community levels of government seem appropriate. On the other hand, the existence of spillovers and income differentials between communities suggests that larger units are needed to internalize the relevant externalities, including fiscal-induced migration, arising as a result of the provision and financing of collective goods and services. Similarly, the existence of economies of scale in at least some urban services also suggests that the conflict in economic criteria for the organization of the optimal governmental unit for local government might be some form of regional government.

When these and other conflicting considerations are taken into account, the optimal form of government structure will likely turn out to be a two-tier or multi-tier structure where some services are provided by the upper tier — either a province or a regional government — and some by the lower tier(s). Indeed, since various forms of most governmental activities consist of a cluster of functions, what appears to be unnecessary overlap of governmental functions may sometimes represent a quite rational solution to the spillover problem. Even complex alignments of responsibilities may thus in some instances be well-defined and well-founded.

ANNEXATION, UNIFICATION, AND TWO-TIER GOVERNMENTS: CANADIAN EXAMPLES

All these and other arguments have frequently been mentioned in the substantial Canadian literature advocating regional governments as a solution to the problems of urban finance. There is little evidence, however, that any serious attempt has been made to quantify the importance of these various offsetting factors or that, in the end, any of these theoretical considerations weighed very heavily in what was done. For example, in Ontario, which has in recent years reorganized almost all its major urban areas into two-tier regional governments, there is no evidence that what little empirical knowledge exists on economies of scale was taken into account in drawing up regional boundaries or in allocating functions between regional and local governments. Indeed, it is difficult to review the many reports on various regional municipalities in Ontario without concluding that economic criteria were not very high in anyone's mind in deciding what to do and how to do it.

Nevertheless, there is no question that the desire to provide urban services more efficiently has been one factor behind the creation of larger government units in many Canadian urban areas, through annexation, unification, and the creation of two-tier or federated municipalities.[20]

Annexation, for example, occurs where one government unit incorporates municipalities in the surrounding area within its geographical boundaries. This form of consolidation results in one jurisdiction providing all of the areawide functions for the consolidated region. Examples of annexation are provided by Calgary, Edmonton, Saint John and St. John's. Since the 1960s, for instance, Calgary — supported by the province — has had a policy of annexing urban areas as well as raw land to the city. Planning in the Calgary area has attempted to help co-ordinate the city with the outlying region and to direct urban growth. Edmonton has also had a policy of annexation but has met with somewhat more resistance than Calgary at bringing in municipalities with a high tax base. Recent annexations in Edmonton, however, have made this city the largest geographically in Canada. Saint John has used annexation since 1967 to increase its geographic size, control urban sprawl, improve transportation, and implement urban renewal. The St. John's Metropolitan Area — a one-tier government — was established in 1960, and its area extended in 1969.

The City of Winnipeg provides an interesting example of *unification*. Growth of the suburbs at the expense of the city in the 1950s led to the formation in 1960 of the Metropolitan Corporation of Greater Winnipeg. This was a two-tier system consisting of twelve municipalities (later reduced to ten) and a metropolitan level of government. The metropolitan corporation was responsible for planning, assessment, arterial roads, water, sewage, parks, flood protection, civil defence, river control, and mosquito abatement. Local governments were left with welfare, police, and fire services. Several studies of this form of government structure found it to be deficient in a number of respects, especially lack of citizen participation and problems with the division of responsibilities and finances. The result of these criticisms was unification, when the City of Winnipeg was formed in 1972. Most services were centralized, with the City of Winnipeg assuming all the major functions of the former thirteen municipalities. To keep up the links with the constituent municipalities, however, twelve community committees were formed. These committees have no legislative authority but serve more as monitoring agencies.

The most common form of government structure in the large cities of Canada today, however, is a *two-tier structure* with either a metropolitan or regional government and lower-tier constituent municipalities. For example, the Montreal Urban Community (MUC), which came into being in 1970, is a federation of thirty municipalities. MUC has responsibility for assessment, planning, food inspection, health, transit, and police. At the request of the constituent municipalities, MUC will also be responsible for air pollution control, central data processing, parks, libraries, housing, and fire services.

The Quebec City Urban Community (QUC) is governed by the same provincial statute as MUC and also came into existence in 1970. It is a federation of twenty-two municipalities of varying size. The upper-tier government is responsible for planning, transit, water purification, assessment, tourist and industrial promotion, and traffic regulations. At the option of the constituent municipalities, QUC will also take charge of water distribution, sewage, garbage, co-ordination of police and fire departments, parks, housing, and libraries.

A two-tier system of local government has also existed in Vancouver since 1967. The federation of fourteen municipalities and three unincorporated districts is known as the Greater Vancouver Regional District (GVRD). The regional district is responsible for regional planning, water and sewage, parks, hospital planning, housing, and the control of air and noise pollution.

The most elaborate system of regional governments has been established in Ontario since the late 1960s. In addition to Metropolitan Toronto, which will be discussed below, the following eleven regional governments were brought into being: Ottawa-Carleton (1969), Niagara (1970), York (1971), Waterloo (1973), Sudbury (1973), Durham (1974), Peel (1974), Halton (1974), Hamilton-Wentworth (1974), Haldimand-Norfolk (1974), and the District Municipality of Muskoka (1971).[21] The regional governments have taken over responsibility for some social and health services, water supply, sewage treatment, garbage disposal, and borrowing. The functions that have remained local are garbage collection, fire protection, parks, and recreation. Some functions are jointly controlled by both levels of government: police, roadways, water distribution, sewer systems, and planning.

As has usually been the case with local government reorganization in Canada, these regional governments were imposed on municipalities by the province and not at the request of the municipalities or their citizens. This background may, in part, account for the apparent general unpopularity of regional governments in Ontario — especially since there are no direct elections to regional councils. In addition, it has been argued that regional governments have resulted in duplication of services and have increased service costs and thus taxes. Where municipalities have been amalgamated or federated, for example, experience suggests that the new uniform service level usually is determined by the municipality with the highest level, thus increasing costs.[22]

Finally, Metropolitan Toronto provides another example of federation. In 1954, thirteen municipalities were amalgamated to form Metropolitan Toronto. Further consolidation took place in 1967, and today there are two cities, five boroughs and a metropolitan corporation, with the division of responsibilities being somewhat similar to that of other regional governments in Ontario. Unlike some of the newer regional governments, the Toronto experiment is generally considered to have been quite successful in terms of service provision, citizen involvement, and other factors.[23]

As these examples suggest, many efforts have been made across Canada to restructure local governments to provide services more efficiently. In particular, the two-tier structure has been used, at least to some extent, to allow those services exhibiting economies of scale and significant spillovers to be provided by the upper-tier government, while allowing the lower-tier governments to provide the remaining services and to encourage citizen access and participation in local decisions. The two-tier structure is certainly one way to deal with the tradeoffs that exist in designing governmental structure. Unfortunately, very little work has been done to test the hypothesis that two-tier structures provide services more efficiently. Are costs higher or lower after amalgamation? Do property taxes go up? Are services duplicated? Is it true that the service levels are "equalized up" to that of the highest service municipalities? These, and other questions, largely remain to be answered.

A POLITICAL ECONOMY PERSPECTIVE

It was noted earlier that the inherent characteristics of public goods (non-rivalness in consumption and nonexcludability) make it difficult to force consumers to reveal their preferences for these goods. In the end, the choice of what quantities of what goods are to be provided can often only be made through the political process. In recent years a substantial literature on what might be called the economic analysis of public choice has been developed.[24] This final section sketches briefly how this "public choice" framework can help to analyze the way in which public goods are actually provided.

Theories of public choice attempt to apply economic analysis to the decisions of politicians, bureaucrats, and citizens. The basic assumption in this approach is that individuals are motivated primarily by self-interest. Each of the three groups mentioned attempts to maximize its own utility or welfare subject to the constraints presented by the behaviour of the other groups. The final outcome, in terms of the quantity of public goods provided, in effect depends on negotiations between these competing groups.

Since individual citizens are assumed to maximize their utility, they will vote for the politicians from whom they expect to receive the highest real income. Individuals have little information on the costs and benefits of various programs and have little incentive to undertake the costly activity needed to acquire this information. Those individuals who have the most to gain and thus do obtain such information may act as lobbyists or form special-interest groups to influence both voters' demands and politicians' choices. The media also have an important role to play both by providing information (true or false) and by influencing citizens and politicians.

Politicians are assumed to maximize their utility as well, where utility is a function of such factors as power and prestige. They will therefore act so as to be sure they receive sufficient votes in order to stay in office. Politicians will therefore tend to supply those public goods that they think citizens want. To the extent that citizens lack information, they will not necessarily demand the quantities of public goods that will make them best off. Also, to the extent that politicians supply what they perceive citizens want (a perception that is also affected by lobbyists), the resulting quantity of public goods provided will not necessarily be efficient.

Finally, government officials or bureaucrats are also assumed to act in their own self-interest and to maximize their utility, which is of course in large part a function of their real income. Since politicians do not know exactly what citizens want, and citizens do not know the costs and benefits of particular programs, bureaucrats can exert significant influence over the output of public goods. They can, for example, restrict output and raise the price of the public good to the government as long as output is not below the amount that would cause citizens to complain. Alternatively, bureaucrats may want to increase the size of their organization and thus their own power and prestige. They can do this by increasing output, but not above the amount for which citizens are willing to pay. To the extent that both citizens and politicians lack information on the optimal quantity of public goods, bureaucratic expansion or restriction of output away from what citizens demand and politicians offer to provide may or may not lead to a more efficient output.

This very brief summary of the public choice literature can readily be applied to the political process at the local level. Citizens within local jurisdictions demand certain local goods and services. Politicians respond to these demands in such a way as to maximize votes. Bureaucrats can also influence the supply of local public goods, largely through their control over information. While there have been some interesting recent attempts to test the relevance of this approach in understanding local expenditure patterns,[25] there is of course still a long way to go before it can be concluded that the "public choice" approach provides the best way to understand what actually happens in the urban public economy.[26] Nevertheless, it is already clear that the more conventional economic literature summarized earlier in this chapter is better at explaining what urban governments *should* do than what they actually do. In the long run, further development of this new "political economy" approach to urban public economics — incorporating, for example, the interplay between provincial and municipal officials and politicians, the voting patterns of homeowners as compared to tenants, et cetera — may prove the key to understanding better the observed patterns of urban expenditures and revenues discussed in the rest of this book.

4 Urban Expenditures

Few subjects have been more discussed in Canada than the enormous growth of government spending in recent decades. From an average of 23 percent of Gross National Expenditure (GNE) in 1947–51, the expenditures of all levels of government rose to an average of 39 percent in 1973–77. Over the postwar period as a whole, total government expenditures as measured in the national accounts rose 73 percent faster than GNE, to the point where the "government expenditure ratio" (total government expenditure as a proportion of GNE) grew to 41 percent in 1978. Government in Canada thus constitutes a large and expanding sector of the economy. Not surprisingly in view of Canada's continued urbanization, local governments have played an important role in this growth.

By level of government, however, it is clear that it is *provincial* expenditures — including those financed by federal transfer payments — that have expanded most rapidly. Over the postwar period as a whole, increased provincial expenditures accounted for 41 percent of the total growth in government expenditures, local (including school) expenditures for 26 percent, and federal expenditures for only 12 percent. The balance is attributable to hospitals and public pension funds. Indeed, in 1978, local governments, according to the national accounts, accounted for only 15 percent of total current government expenditure in Canada. This figure is in some ways misleading, however, because so much of the expenditure of the other two levels of government consists of intergovernmental transfer payments. In 1977, for example, the federal government transferred $9.6 billion to the provincial governments and $0.4 billion to local governments, while in turn provincial governments transferred $8.5 billion to local governments (including schools) and another $6.0 billion to hospitals.

As a result of these massive intergovernmental fiscal transfers, it is at the local and hospital levels that increased "exhaustive" expenditures (government purchases of goods and services) — the only part of government spending that actually "uses up" the nation's resources — were most important over the last decade, accounting for 80 percent of the total expenditure increases in this sector from 1968 to 1977. By 1977, local governments accounted for 34 percent of total government expenditure on goods and services, and such expenditures, including capital expenditures, accounted for 92 percent of local expenditures.[1] In dollar terms, local governments (including schools) spent $17.2 billion on goods and services in 1977, compared to only $14.6 billion for the provinces, and $12.2 billion for the federal government.

In terms of employment too, the local government sector is extremely important. In 1975, for example, the municipal government sector, broadly defined to include schools and municipal enterprises, employed about 705,000 Canadians and accounted for 33 percent of all public civilian employees and almost 8 percent of *all* employment in Canada in that year. In contrast, total federal civilian employment, including public enterprises, was only 462,000, and total provincial employment, again including public enterprises, was only 626,000, excluding hospitals — though provincial employment was 996,000 if all hospital employees were included.[2]

The municipal sector in Canada is therefore very important both as a spender and an employer in addition to being (as mentioned in chapter 2) probably the most important direct supplier of publicly provided goods and services to Canadians. The next section explores the pattern of urban expenditures in a little more detail, and the remainder of the present chapter considers, first, some factors affecting the growth of such expenditures and, second, some possible ways of improving the efficiency with which cities spend taxpayers' money.

THE PATTERN OF LOCAL EXPENDITURES

Table 4-1 breaks down local government expenditure functions by province for 1978. Although there are variations between provinces, by far the largest proportion of local expenditures is for education (42.1 percent for all local governments), followed by transportation and communications (11.6 percent), "fiscal services," a category that includes debt charges and transfers to reserves and own enterprises (9.6 percent), environment (8.6 percent), and protection of persons and property (7.5 percent). If education, which is provided by separate school boards, is left out of account, the most important urban expenditures, in municipalities over 50,000, in terms of employment, are protection, recreation, public works, and general government. Together these traditional local government activities accounted for over four-fifths of all noneducational local employment in Canada's largest municipalities in 1975.[3]

Many examples of provincial variation in local expenditure responsibilities can be found in Table 4-1, apart from the obvious variation in the levels of per capita expenditure. As noted previously, for example, education is entirely a provincial responsibility in New Brunswick. Almost no expenditures are made by local governments on health in Newfoundland, New Brunswick, Prince Edward Island, and Quebec, but health is an important local function in Saskatchewan (13.6 percent of total local expenditures) and Alberta (14.9 percent). Social welfare expenditures are not made by local governments in Newfoundland, Prince Edward Island, New Brunswick, and the Territories, but local welfare expenditures make up 9.6 percent of total local expenditures in Nova Scotia and 6.0 percent in Ontario.

TABLE 4-1

General Local Government Expenditure by Province, 1978
(as percent of total)

Functions	NFLD	PEI	NS	NB	QUE.	ONT.	MAN.	SASK.	ALTA.	BC	YUKON	NWT	TOTAL
General Government	10.2	1.9	4.0	5.9	6.9	3.9	3.2	3.8	3.2	3.6	9.7	14.4	4.6
Protection of persons & property	4.7	3.0	7.2	18.8	7.4	7.9	7.9	6.1	5.8	8.3	7.6	3.0	7.5
Transportation & Communications	21.5	3.3	6.4	29.4	11.1	11.6	12.2	13.8	13.9	8.9	14.6	19.3	11.6
Environment	28.6	5.4	7.5	21.1	9.2	7.6	6.8	6.6	10.3	8.7	49.6	24.5	8.6
Health	0.1	–	5.0	–	0.1	5.2	8.9	13.6	14.9	0.9	0.6	0.3	4.9
Social Services – Social Welfare	–	–	9.6	–	0.3	6.0	1.2	0.8	1.0	1.2	–	–	3.0
Regional Planning & Development	1.1	0.7	0.9	1.5	0.5	1.1	1.4	0.8	2.2	1.6	2.7	12.5	1.1
Housing, general assistance	0.1	5.0	–	0.1	0.2	0.2	–	–	0.5	–	2.2	0.7	0.2
Resource Conservation & Industrial Development	0.2	–	0.2	0.9	0.2	1.3	0.5	0.2	2.1	0.2	0.3	0.1	0.8
Recreation & Culture	7.7	2.9	3.1	10.1	5.0	6.2	5.6	6.3	6.6	7.1	6.5	7.4	5.9
Education, primary & secondary	7.6	72.7	48.3	–	47.4	41.2	42.7	41.0	30.4	46.6	–	14.0	42.1
Fiscal Services	18.1	5.1	7.6	12.0	11.6	7.8	9.6	7.0	9.1	12.9	6.2	3.8	9.6
Other Services	0.1	–	0.2	0.2	0.1	–	–	–	–	–	–	–	0.1
General Expenditure	100.0	100.0	100.0	100.0	100.0	100.0	100.0	100.0	100.0	100.0	100.0	100.0	100.0
Expenditure per capita ($)	201	658	771	260	1016	1033	895	991	1372	941	631	888	984

SOURCES: Statistics Canada, *Local Government Finance, 1978.*

TABLE 4-2

General Expenditure, Selected Cities, 1977
(as percent of total)

Function	Montreal	Quebec	Hamilton-Wentworth	Ottawa-Carleton	Toronto	Winnipeg	Calgary	Edmonton	Vancouver
General Government	7.2	8.3	2.9	4.6	3.8	6.0	2.9	2.9	3.4
Protection of persons & property	11.8	8.5	9.6	7.8	11.5	9.7	8.8	8.3	11.4
Transportation & Communications	14.7	10.8	11.0	11.8	8.3	12.3	12.0	12.5	7.2
Environment	11.7	10.2	7.2	5.4	7.9	6.8	7.7	9.3	7.5
Health	.2	–	13.9	13.8	1.8	2.7	14.9	10.1	1.1
Social Services – Social Welfare	.8	.2	6.1	5.2	6.4	2.0	1.4	1.5	1.8
Housing, general assistance	1.8	.8	1.5	2.2	.7	.9	1.2	.8	3.4
Natural resources	–	–	–	.1	–	.3	–	–	–
Agriculture, trade & industry & tourism	.2	.3	–	.4	–	–	1.9	–	–
Recreation & culture	4.7	7.6	5.1	5.7	6.6	6.0	7.6	10.0	7.4
Education, primary & secondary	33.8	41.0	33.0	33.6	42.5	42.2	32.2	33.4	45.7
Fiscal Services	13.1	12.2	9.2	9.3	10.3	10.9	9.5	10.3	10.1
Other Services	–	–	.3	–	.2	.3	–	.9	1.0
General Expenditure	100.0	100.0	100.0	100.0	100.0	100.0	100.0	100.0	100.0
Expenditure per capita ($)	1,158	957	1,041	1,172	1,024	869	1,309	1,286	905

SOURCES: Statistics Canada, *Local Government Finance 1977 and 1978*.

Although local governments in all provinces make expenditures on transportation and communications, the size of these expenditures varies from a low of 3.3 percent of total local expenditure in Prince Edward Island to a high of 29.4 percent in New Brunswick. Expenditures on protection (fire and police) range from a low of 4.7 percent of total local expenditures in Newfoundland to a high of 18.8 percent in New Brunswick. Again, these percentages are higher in New Brunswick because education is not included as a local expenditure.

Table 4-2 provides a similar breakdown of expenditures for nine major Canadian cities in 1977. The highest per capita local expenditures were in Calgary ($1309) and Edmonton ($1286), and the lowest were in Winnipeg ($869). In all cities, the largest expenditure category, by far, was again education, which ranged from 45.7 percent of total local expenditures in Vancouver to 32.2 percent in Calgary. Health expenditures generally appear to be a far more important function for large cities than for the small cities, accounting for over 10 percent of total local expenditures in Hamilton-Wentworth, Ottawa-Carleton, Calgary, and Edmonton. Finally, expenditures per capita in each of these large cities exceed their respective provincial averages. This point is further emphasized by the functional breakdown in Table 4-3. It appears that the level of expenditures varies directly with the size of cities — partly because urban areas provide more or better services, and partly because urban areas have a greater number of highly paid employees.[4] The differences in expenditure levels shown in Table 4-3 for the provision of health and housing probably reflect mainly the first of these factors, while those for the provision of protection and general government reflect the latter.

Table 4-3 also shows the wide divergence in the extent to which local expenditures are paid for out of local revenues rather than provincial or federal grants. In total, only 54.5 percent of local expenditures are financed locally, but the proportion is much higher for the "traditional" local expenditures — protection, transportation, environment, and recreation. As shown in the table and discussed in chapter 7, most transfers received by local governments are targeted to specific expenditure functions, particularly education.

Finally, Table 4-3 shows that education expenditures, even though they are heavily supported by provincial transfers, constitute by far the largest single drain on local revenues. Except for New Brunswick, where education is entirely financed by the province, and Prince Edward Island and Newfoundland, where grants finance almost all local educational expenditures,[5] local taxes finance a substantial fraction of education, and these education taxes account for a substantial fraction of local taxes. Because of its importance and the special administrative arrangements for education in most provinces, this important aspect of local government activity is treated separately in chapter 6.

TABLE 4-3

Local Per Capita Expenditures from Own-source Revenues, by Function, 1977

Function	Percent of Local Expenditures Financed from Own Sources	All Local Governments	Urban Regions	Urban as % Total
General Government	85.4	33.41	37.94	114
Protection	85.4	57.48	75.22	131
Transportation	70.5	73.61	92.23	125
Health	14.5	5.35	17.81	333
Social Services	47.1	12.07	–	–
Education	31.5	122.28	128.60	105
Resources	57.9	4.38	4.71	108
Environment	82.6	65.31	66.48	102
Recreation	77.1	42.34	46.94	111
Housing	54.5	6.79	20.71	305
Other	80.1	69.03	71.62	104
Total	54.5	492.05	562.26	114

SOURCE: Harry Kitchen, "Municipal Finance in Canada" (to be published by Canadian Tax Foundation).

So far as the remaining local expenditures are concerned, the most important points to note are: (1) the continuing dominance of such traditional local functions as police and fire protection, roads, and recreation; and (2) the generally higher level of expenditures on all functions in urban areas. As a proportion of total locally funded expenditures, excluding education, the fastest growth over the 1968–77 period was in recreation, but protection continued to be by far the largest expenditure item. In addition, as noted earlier, protection, like education, is a very labor-intensive activity and accounts for a very high proportion of local employment (over 30 percent in 1975). The labor-intensive nature of many local services has, indeed, been seen by many as a key factor explaining the growth of local expenditure in recent years, as discussed in the next section.

THE GROWTH OF LOCAL EXPENDITURES

Fifteen years ago William Baumol (1967) suggested that differential productivity growth in different sectors of the economy might account for some of the growth in the relative size of the public sector. Bradford, Malt, and Oates (1969) subsequently suggested that the U.S. local public sector in particular had expanded at least in part because it was inherently labor intensive and hence had a low rate of productivity growth. Auld (1976a) made a similar suggestion with respect to Canada. The Baumol argument hinges on the fact that, with productivity rising more slowly in the public than in the private sector, a rising proportion of national resources has to flow into the public sector in order to maintain even a constant level of public services. Given the linkage through the labor market of wages in the public and private sectors, unit employment costs — and hence government expenditure — must therefore rise in order to purchase a constant level of real resources. This argument suggests that since subnational levels of government likely provide generally labor-intensive services, their relative importance should rise over time.

There is no shortage of contradictory hypotheses in the field of government expenditure growth, however. In contrast to the "Baumol hypothesis" that public activities are labor intensive, De Alessi (1969) suggested that they instead tend to be capital intensive, essentially because bureaucrats and politicians are interested in receiving the benefits from their actions during their tenure and therefore tend to use excessively low discount rates and build too many excessively large "monuments." Others too have frequently noted the apparent bias in public-sector projects towards grandiose designs as monuments to politicians. Large sums are occasionally spent on the construction of projects with little being allotted to the efficient running of the service once it is instituted. The career of a politician or government official may be enhanced by the construction of a particular project, but it does not seem to depend as much on whether or not the project functions well on an everyday basis. De Alessi's idea received some apparent support in a study by Orzechowski (1974), who found that the capital to worker ratio was exceptionally high in the United States federal public sector.

In contrast, the Baumol hypothesis was supported by Bradford, Malt, and Oates (1969), who noted that the financing problems that American local municipalities faced in the area of capital expenditures — for which they would normally have to go to the electorate on a bond referendum — tended to make the utilization of factors more labor intensive than would otherwise have been the case. For institutional reasons, however, one might perhaps expect the opposite result in Canada. For the most part, capital expenditures on schools, for example, have been financed almost entirely by provincial governments through special capital funds, while significant components of the current costs have been raised by local property taxes. Provincial controls on municipal capital expenditures (see chapter 2) and provincial capital grants (see chapter 7) also influence municipal capital expenditures in various ways. On the whole, one might expect there to be a strong propensity on the part of Canadian local governments to substitute capital for labor, contrary to what one might expect from a simple application of the Baumol hypothesis.

Several sources of evidence may be brought to bear on these questions.[6] On the wages side, for example, national accounts data show that civilian government wages as a proportion of total civilian expenditure on goods and services have indeed risen in the postwar period, with the fastest rise taking place in the 1960s. These data also suggest, however, that this rise has not been particularly smooth, and that it seems to have ceased in the 1970s. The Baumol hypothesis thus receives some, but not very strong, support from this source.

In fact, public-sector activities in general appear to have been much more capital intensive than nonpublic-sector activities, thus lending support to the De Alessi hypothesis. In 1975, for example, on average, about twice as much capital was employed per worker in the public sector as in the private sector. Throughout the postwar period, however, the capital per worker in the public sector, however defined, has declined steadily in relation to that in the economy as a whole. That is, the public sector has become increasingly labor intensive in recent decades, a fact that lends considerable support to the Baumol hypothesis. The only alternative explanation that comes to mind — a postwar "capital boom" making up for the wartime deficit and then being worked down to a "norm" — is rather hard to swallow.

The relative labor intensity of the different components of the public sector has changed somewhat during the postwar period, with the education and hospital sectors, always much more labor intensive than government proper, becoming even more so in recent years. Interestingly, however, while the same increase in labor intensity is observable, the provincial-municipal sector in general has remained consistently the *least* labor-intensive part of the public sector as a whole, and indeed, less labor intensive than either the industrial or service sectors as a whole — in some contrast to the common (Baumol) view that they are more labor intensive.

On the whole, then, the evidence relating the observed growth of urban expenditures to the labor intensity of local public services is at best mixed. A much more convincing explanation accounting for this expenditure growth has been inflation, both in general and in public-sector wages in particular. Over the 1966–76 period, for example, approximately 78 percent of the total increase in provincial-local expenditure has been attributed to inflation. Of the balance, 4 percent reflects population growth and the remaining 18 percent presumably reflects increases in the level of services.[7]

In part, inflation has had so strong an impact on public-sector expenditures because of the so-called "relative price effect," by which is meant the fact that the prices of the goods and services purchased by government have grown relatively faster than the general price level, particularly since 1965. Nominal public expenditures thus had to grow simply to secure the same level of inputs and, if productivity is unchanged, to provide an unchanged level of public services. In other words, the results are the same as in the Baumol case, but the mechanism envisaged to be at work is quite different, arising from a relative increase in the prices of public-sector inputs rather than an increase in private-sector productivity and wages leading to an increase in public wages through the operations of an integrated labor market.

Governments have not been slow in pointing to inflation to explain away much of the growth in the public sector, or at least to demonstrate that this growth was out of their hands.[8] Basically, however, this argument is rather specious. No law compels governments to maintain constant the level and mix of inputs they purchase. The decision to continue with existing programs in the face of rising costs is inherently political. Furthermore, since the major item purchased by government is labor, the main reason for the relative price effect is that the price of the labor purchased by government is rising — and that other factors are not being substituted for the now more expensive labor. From 1967 to 1977, for example, the base wages paid by local governments rose on average 10.6 percent annually compared to a 9.6 percent increase in the private sector. On average, municipal wages for at least some categories of workers appear to have risen more than private wages throughout the 1960s and 1970s.

The extent to which wage determination in the public sector is out of the hands of government is of course arguable, as is the possibility of substituting capital or other inputs for relatively more expensive labor in government production. In both instances, however, it would surely be going too far to assign government a totally passive role. Governments as a whole thus not only consciously decide to maintain the real level of their activities, they are also not completely innocent of responsibility for the existence and size of the relative price effect in the first place. This point is obviously not so significant for any individual city, which must compete for skilled labor against other governments at all levels as well as the private sector. From a city's viewpoint, it is thus probably generally correct to view the relative price effect as something they simply have to live with. Consequently, most of urban expenditure growth can indeed legitimately be interpreted as reflecting mainly inflationary forces beyond local control.

It should perhaps be noted, finally, that all this has nothing necessarily to do with the level of public-sector *output*. Even if the real cost of government inputs remains constant over time, it is not possible to say whether output also remains constant, goes down, or increases. Input data alone tell us nothing about productivity unless one is willing to make the strong assumption that output varies directly with input — an assumption made implicitly in the national accounts, or in the Baumol approach discussed above — or that output remains constant over time, even though inputs vary. The problem of public productivity is discussed briefly in the next section.

IMPROVING EXPENDITURE EFFICIENCY

Urban governments can probably do little, at least individually, about such broad forces affecting their expenditures as discussed in the last section.

What any city can do, however, is to use the resources available to it as efficiently as possible. This section therefore discusses briefly some issues affecting the efficiency with which public expenditures are carried out.

Suggestions to limit or to radically restructure governments in order to restrain their growth and to ensure that resources that flow through the public sector are used efficiently are today heard on all sides. These suggestions may be divided into two broad classes: those intended to alter political institutions and those intended to alter bureaucratic incentive structures. Despite the propensity of some proponents of such changes to overstate their merits and probable results, there is, in principle, a good deal of merit in many of these proposals.

Reducing fiscal illusion through employing user charges, for example, is clearly desirable on broad democratic grounds and may indeed have substantial effects on urban public efficiency, as elaborated in chapter 6. Proposals to increase controls imposed on the decisions made by public officials, for example, through limiting tax rates, are not necessarily costless, however. It can be argued equally well that to get the greatest benefit out of resources channeled through the public sector — and perhaps even to ensure that we employ only those resources in the public sector that can be efficiently used there — we should provide much greater freedom and incentive for efficiency and innovation to managers in the public sector.

There are three ways to bring together the motivations and actions of public servants with those of citizens in general: through the "market system," the "threat system," or the "integrative system." Reliance on the integrative system — on the sharing of responsibility and a sense of belonging to a common community — although the base on which Utopian schemes have been constructed through history, has a relatively dismal record in practice. The right things should of course be said, and expected, of public officials, but it would be naïve to rely on shared values alone to produce the desired results.

The presumed inability of the market system to function satisfactorily in the public sector has therefore led many to rely not on the altruism of public servants but rather on their fear in an effort to control their actions — through, for example, such measures as banning strikes. This use of threats, however, also seems a rather unsatisfactory solution. A good deal of experience suggests that if people behave in a certain way only because they are threatened with dire consequences if they do not so behave, then one is not likely to get a very good level of service. In fact, those thus threatened are able to rationalize all sorts of misbehavior precisely on the grounds that they are acting under duress.[9]

If neither the integrative nor the threat mechanisms are particularly useful in the public sector, then it appears that we must rely more on the market mechanism. Many common proposals to improve efficiency follow this path. Werner Hirsch (1978), for example, has suggested that the job security of public employees be reduced by altering civil service laws, by increasing contracting out, by separating functions in vertically integrated departments, and so on. The basic idea of such changes is to alter the incentives facing civil servants in order to ensure more sensitivity to the desires of consumers. A different approach might be to enlarge the value of nonmonetary awards, through devices such as introducing a British-type honor system, allowing more explicit use of professional titles and authorship rights, stressing such social incentives as "team spirit," and so on. Experiments with such devices as productivity bargaining, payment by results, and fixed-output contracts might also help in some areas.

Obviously, none of these devices would resolve all problems, and some would not be at all suitable in particular areas, but each would probably help somewhere. If payment by results were really feasible, for example, the activity in question could probably as well be carried out in the private sector anyway. Nevertheless, it is probably along these lines that "solutions," if any exist, seem most likely to be found.

The solution most commonly put forth in public-sector problems, however — simply to improve the efficiency and effectiveness with which government spends taxpayers' money — is likely one of the most unworkable in practice. No critic of government has ever failed to point out many ways in which the government — any government — could carry out its activities both more efficiently in terms of using fewer resources to achieve the same outcomes and more effectively in terms of using the same resources to achieve more desired outcomes. What is seldom brought out in such diatribes, however, is the extreme difficulty, in the context of government, of implementing efficiency and effectiveness measures. So ingrained in the governmental system are these difficulties that it is unlikely that any solution to them will be found in the near future.

Municipal budgeting and expenditure analysis could doubtless be greatly improved through the introduction of such techniques of rational expenditure analysis as the PPB (Planning Programming Budgeting) system. Robinson (1971), for example, urged the widespread adoption of this technique by Canadian municipalities. More recently, ZBB (Zero-Based Budgeting) has also been put forth as a panacea to local expenditure problems.[10] There is no question that most Canadian municipalities could improve the efficiency and effectiveness of their activities through adopting these and other practices of rational expenditure evaluation. It is clearly better to define the objectives of policy carefully, to cost and compare adequately the programs intended to achieve those objectives, and to evaluate the effectiveness of the programs adopted than not to do so.

At a more fundamental level, however, such techniques can only go so far for two reasons: (1) the difficulty of measuring the output of government in the first place; and (2) the lack of incentive for anyone in the governmental structure to increase outputs, however measured. The first of these problems may not be as insuperable as is often thought.[11] The second problem, however, may be. Not only is it necessary to have a strong commitment from the top in order to overcome inertia and objections from below, but it is also necessary to structure the incentives facing both top decision makers and those who actually implement policies in order to achieve the desired results. Neither of these things is very easy to do. This is not to say that municipal finances cannot be more rationally controlled and evaluated than is typically the case, but just to caution that great progress cannot be expected quickly in altering long-standing practices in this or other respects.

Moreover, a point that has too often been lost sight of in the discussion of public spending is that such spending is not an end in itself. The central concern of any sensible citizen must still be with what government activity actually means for him. In this sense, it is not clear that increasing control over the details of expenditure will or can do much to improve the rationality of government spending decisions. What such increased control may do is to reduce the number of such decisions and to delay those that are made — a result that is unlikely to add much, if anything, to the well-being of most individuals. It may, moreover, make the bureaucratic environment even less attractive to able decision makers, thus lowering the general quality of whatever the public sector ends up doing.

Organizational Reform

A somewhat similar predicament arises with respect to the frequent proposals to resolve local problems by reorganizing local governments (see chapter 3). Journalists, citizens, and many academics seem to take it as an article of faith that it is always desirable to reduce duplication and overlapping in the public sector in the name, for example, of administrative efficiency and cost-saving. Another important argument against duplication and overlapping is that the resulting confusion weakens accountability substantially and subjects groups to different conflicting and confusing policies.

"Co-ordination," however, is one of those "good" words that, when examined closely, in fact need not have good connotations in the context of government activity. In economics, it is usually called "collusion," and has a somewhat different connotation! Increased co-ordination, for example, generally means increased *coercion*, in the sense that someone's or some central agency's will is imposed on someone else's will, with no possible presumption that it is necessarily better. It will be recalled, for example, that a central economic argument for local governments in the first place is that decentralized provision of many services is superior to centralized provision precisely because it can better reflect local differences.

Moreover, a more centralized and co-ordinated system is not necessarily a more reliable system. It is an accepted proposition in the design of mechanical devices — as in nature's design of biological devices — that a certain amount of redundancy is necessary to achieve an acceptable degree of *reliability*. Also, the more uncertain the environment within which an organism or an organization must function, the greater the importance of its reliability. If, as most would presumably accept, government is an essential element of life in a modern complex society, then this suggests that the ideal governmental system must contain a fair amount of redundancy (excess capacity) in order to achieve the necessary minimal degree of reliability needed for the maintenance of our modern industrial life-style.

As Landau (1969, p. 356) put this case: "If there is no duplication, if there is no overlap, if there is no ambiguity, an organization will neither be able to suppress error nor generate alternative routes of action." Redundancy is nature's way of suppressing error, of enabling an organism or, by analogy, an organization to function reliably in the face of error. Redundancy thus leads to reliability. Reliability in turn means that an organization is more adaptable to changing circumstances. And adaptability in turn means that an organization will tend to be more "efficient" in the long run.

In other words, an organizational structure of government that is full of duplication and overlap — in which, for example, the jurisdiction of various parts of government is highly uncertain — may prove to be a more efficient form of organization in the long run than a rigidly structured, tidy organization. Duplication may thus in some instances be a control device to reduce the misallocation and inefficiency almost inherent in the bureaucratic supply of public goods. To the extent that this is true, it follows that the consolidation of previously separate governmental functions or governmental jurisdictions will usually tend to increase expenditure because the resulting unit will be more monopolistic, with fewer competitive incentives and higher monitoring costs (see also chapter 3).

Sometimes instead of consolidating local government services into geographically larger jurisdictions, an opposite approach to improving efficiency is followed, by fragmenting such services into functionally separate special commissions, boards, and enterprises. Such independent public services are sometimes thought to be generally well run, honest, and efficient, while services run as part of the political structure are likely to be worse in all of these respects. The proliferation of separate school boards, police commissions, water, telephone, and electrical utilities characterizing the urban public sector in most larger Canadian cities suggests that the idea that many public services are too important to be left to "politics" has had some influence. In Metropolitan Toronto, for example, there are over 100 local special-purpose authorities. The growth of "supramunicipal" authorities — regional governments et cetera — at least partly insulated from direct political contact with constituents through the ballot box leads to much the same conclusion.

In reality, however, there is little research that supports the proposition that relatively autonomous public-service organizations are in any sense better or more efficient than organizational structures that are more directly politically responsible. The characteristic incentive structure of an autonomous public utility, for example, is likely to be such as to reduce or avoid feedback from the public (consumers) other than that which supports its own organizational goals — such as expansion on the one hand and a "quiet life" on the other. Removing the provision of a number of urban public services at least partly from the political arena probably has some effect in reducing the possible use of those services for such "political" reasons as reducing conflict between different groups. Whether this is necessarily a desirable outcome is less clear, particularly when a price is usually paid in terms of reducing the control that the responsible political authorities can exercise over the level and pattern of expenditures. In one of the few Canadian studies on this issue, for example, Kitchen (1975, 1977) found the per unit cost of supplying water through a separate water or utilities commission was greater than the cost of supply by a department directly responsible to city council, in part because of weaker pressures toward public accountability. Once again, as was the case with regional government (see chapter 3), the results of such "functional fragmentation" of the provision of urban services into a series of quasi-autonomous entities may in practice turn out to be quite different from what appears to be commonly expected.[12]

Limits to Competition

Even where competition — whether between public and private or competing public providers — is feasible, it may have undesirable consequences in the public sector. The essence of competition is that dissatisfied clients have an option to go elsewhere for their services. The lack of this option for many public services is in fact why the public sector may have little incentive to provide the service in an efficient manner, that is, according to consumer preferences. Having nowhere else to go, the client must accept the way the services are provided, or do without them, if that is possible. Providing alternatives, however, means that the dissatisfied clientele may seek the alternatives rather than trying to improve the existing public services.

If inefficiencies occur in the public sector because of the absence of competition, an obvious solution might be to allow elements of competition whenever feasible, for example, through decentralization and interdepartmental competition, or through contracting with the private sector whenever feasible, to serve as a bench mark or standard to measure whether the public sector is providing the services efficiently.

Policies of encouraging competition may also, of course, give rise to problems. Many public-sector activities exist precisely because market imperfections and failures are such that private, unregulated markets will not provide the socially optimal amount of certain goods and services. Even in the context of the Tiebout model developed in chapter 3, where differing communities compete in providing different mixes of services, while the threat of exit may improve the provision of the services, conditions might also be improved by citizen criticism and protest. Indeed, the very persons who "vote with their feet" are probably those who could do most to improve the existing system through various forms of "voice". The possibility of exit may thus create a two-tier system, with the wealthy leaving for expensive private services (for example, private schools and hospitals, private security systems in the suburbs), and the poor having to remain with declining public services. While such a system may be efficient in the narrow sense that people get what they pay for, it may not be equitable. In the long run it may certainly be a sensible alternative for a society to opt for a less efficient but more equitable public-sector delivery system.

As this example suggests, ultimately in the public sector it must be the political process that serves as the constraining influence to ensure administrative efficiency in the provision of public services. The political process therefore is to the public sector what profits and competition are to the private sector. The political process seldom has a direct impact in achieving efficiency in the public sector; rather, its impact is usually indirect as decisions are made to alter the institutional framework within which the public sector operates. Thus the political process is the ultimate impetus for policies to improve the incentive structure facing politicians and bureaucrats, to utilize basic economic principles of efficiency, and to encourage competition and "voice" in the public sector.

In the private sector, consumer preferences are registered through purchases — dollar votes — with dissatisfied customers going elsewhere for their purchases. In the public sector, consumer preferences are ultimately registered by votes at the ballot box, or by "voting with one's feet." While each of these solutions does provide an ultimate constraint, each also has problems associated with it.

Registering preferences through votes, for example, is exceedingly cumbersome. Not only are the opportunities infrequent, but also one usually has to vote for a package — in the extreme, one votes for a political party that may have as one element of its platform some policies designed to encourage administrative efficiency in the public sector.

Voting with one's feet (the Tiebout model) involves moving to an area that provides the package of public goods and corresponding taxes that best approximate the preferences of the individuals making the move. This approximation to a market solution through the threat of exit may induce a degree of administrative efficiency as cities risk losing their tax base if they do not provide an administratively efficient delivery system.

Again, however, the process is exceedingly blunt and costly, and often involves a choice only amongst broad packages, rather than specific items. In addition, as noted above, the exit option reduces voice, again often from the very people who could best improve the system.

In spite of these problems with the political constraint, more consideration should be given to making this constraint workable, since it is the ultimate force that can be relied upon to induce efficiency in public-sector management. Decentralization — the opposite of regionalization — can help put issues closer to voters. More use of charges (see chapter 6) can help highlight the cost of public services; independent, external financial audits can disclose gross inefficiencies; and improved measures of performance can help voters make judicious choices. Most important, perhaps, is to ensure that the various elements of the public sector are ultimately accountable through the political process — or at least that the public has some recourse through the political process (through voice and ultimately votes) to register satisfaction or dissatisfaction with the way in which public services are provided — and that this most basic of public choices is exercised in as informed a manner as possible. This idea is further developed with respect to education in chapter 6.

Given the problems with increasing competition and exit in the public sector, an obvious alternative is to encourage voice as a way of improving public services. The media may play a potentially important role in this area by providing a vehicle for the dissatisfied to "go public." Complaint columns, for example, can be a potent source of embarrassment to the public sector and to those who are ultimately responsible politically. Likewise, the threat of an adverse editorial, or letter to the editor can be a powerful check on the public and private sectors alike. One of the most important instruments for ensuring the accountability and responsiveness of urban governments is therefore an independent, questioning, local newspaper or other media.

Control of governmental efficiency by voice has its own problems, however, largely because it has the characteristics of a "public good," as defined in chapter 3. That is, the benefits of voice that lead to improvement in public services go to all users of the public services. The costs, however, are often borne only by the persons who complain. Even small issues such as complaining about poor public service or about inadequate facilities take time and effort, especially if the providers of the service are able to make the responsibility diffuse and to block channels of complaint. (How many people have sworn to write a letter of complaint, only to let it pass when they were not sure whom to write to or when they became too busy with other things?) More serious forms of voice may be even costlier in personal terms; direct appeals to the public may lead to a loss of job, and blacklisting; reporting rape may lead to social stigma and hostile treatment in the courts; active protest may lead to the imposition of criminal sanctions; and even reporting crimes may lead to costly time spent in courts and possible retaliation by criminals. One cannot blame individuals for failing to bear such costs when the benefits are spread throughout society at large. The incentive structure is not always such as to encourage the socially optimal amount of voice.

To be sure, policies can be designed to reduce the private costs and to increase the private benefits of voice. In some cases, for example, preserving the anonymity of complainants may reduce the costs, while rewards, monetary or otherwise, can increase the private benefits. Similarly, an ombudsman can go a long way towards reducing private costs by pursuing the case for an aggrieved individual and by opening up channels of communication. (Most such "solutions," it should be noted, involve *higher* public expenditures and employment.)

There is little incentive for public officials to take steps to establish appropriate channels for voice and lines of communication. In fact, there is generally a perverse incentive for them to discourage communications, since voice can make matters uncomfortable for those in the public sector. Whereas firms in the private sector can sometimes gain from voice — it can tell them where to improve services and hence reduce exit and loss of customers — public-sector agencies may actually prefer a reduction in clientele to the extent that it reduces workloads and complaints without affecting budgets!

Conclusion

In summary, while most simplistic views of the causes and consequences of public sector growth are without foundation, there is reason to think that at least some elements of this growth may have exceeded that which would have been socially desirable. The question therefore arises of how we are to prevent the further development of such aberrations in the future. While there is no real solution, greater openness and information both on the nature of government activities and on the reasoning and studies underlying government policies is clearly a necessary ingredient. To improve information about government, public agencies at all levels should be forced to publicize in detail the reasoning underlying the various actions that they take, or do not take.

To have good government, it must operate in a fishbowl. Most bureaucrats and politicians will obviously not like such conditions. Nevertheless, without a public better informed of the real alternatives and choices facing them in their collective capacity as members of society, it is hard to believe that the outcome of the urban political process — the process by which the level and mix of public-sector activities are inevitably determined — can become much "better" than it now is.

5 Urban Revenues

The next three chapters discuss various aspects of urban revenue systems in some detail. After an overview of the pattern of urban revenues, the remainder of chapter 5 discusses the major "own-source" revenue of Canadian municipalities, the property tax, in some detail and concludes with a brief look at such alternative sources of revenues as local income and sales taxes. Chapter 6 is devoted to pricing urban services, an aspect of urban finance that has not been well developed in Canada, but where the potential for future expansion seems considerable. This chapter also contains a discussion of some important issues in the financing of education, which constitutes the largest drain on local revenues at the present time. Finally, chapter 7 considers the nature and effects of the provincial grants that have come to constitute such an important source of municipal revenues in recent years.

THE PATTERN OF REVENUES

As chapter 4 notes with respect to expenditures, the provincial governments have in recent years constituted the most important level of government with respect to revenues. In 1978, for example, the provinces accounted for 40 percent of total revenues collected by the public sector, compared to 33 percent for the federal government, 17 percent for local governments, and 10 percent for "other" (hospitals, pension funds). The proportion of revenues collected by local governments has fallen significantly over the last decade — from 18.5 percent in 1968 to 16.7 percent in 1978. Again, this relative decline parallels what we saw on the expenditure side in chapter 4.

   The composition of local government revenues has also changed over time, as is shown in Table 5–1. "Own-source" revenues are largely composed of property taxes but also include grants in lieu of taxes, sales of goods and services, rentals, concessions and franchises, licences and permits, remittances from own enterprises, interest, interest and penalties on taxes, fines, and other miscellaneous revenues. Transfers come largely from the provincial government, with a few federal government transfers amounting to less than one percent of total revenues. Transfers can be either general purpose (used for any purpose) or specific purpose (used for a specific purpose prescribed by the donor government). The role of transfers in local fiscal decisions is discussed in chapter 7.

TABLE 5-1

Local Government Revenue, 1967-80
(percent)

Year	Own-Source Revenue		Transfers
	Property Taxes	Other	
1967	46.0	13.9	40.1
1968	46.2	13.3	40.5
1969	45.9	12.3	41.8
1970	44.3	12.2	43.5
1971	42.2	11.1	46.7
1972	41.9	11.6	46.5
1973	40.4	13.0	46.6
1974	38.5	13.1	48.4
1975	37.3	12.9	49.8
1976	38.5	13.4	48.1
1977	37.7	13.7	48.6
1978	37.8	14.5	47.7
1979[a]	36.8	14.1	49.1
1980[b]	38.7	15.4	45.9

SOURCE: Statistics Canada, *Local Government Finance* (various years).

[a] Preliminary
[b] Estimates

The importance of intergovernmental transfers has changed somewhat over the last decade as is shown in Table 5-1. Transfers have been steadily increasing from 40.1 percent of local revenues in 1967 to 45.9 percent in 1980. There has been a concomitant decline in own-source revenues from 59.9 percent in 1967 to 54.1 percent in 1980. This decrease likely reflects in part the decline in popularity of the local property tax (see next section). Although revenues from own sources still provide slightly over one-half of total local government revenues in most provinces, as with expenditure responsibilities, there is considerable variation from province to province.

Table 5-2 shows the revenue sources for local governments by province for 1978. Revenues from own sources as a proportion of total revenues for local governments in the country as a whole were 52.3 percent, with transfers accounting for the remaining 47.7 percent. Revenues from own sources ranged from a low of 14.7 percent of total local revenues in Prince Edward Island to a high of 66.8 percent in British Columbia. In six provinces, more than half of total revenues came from own sources. The largest component of local own-source revenues is the property tax, which provided close to 40 percent of total local revenues in the country as a whole, and a comparably significant share in every province except PEI. In British

TABLE 5-2

Distribution of General Local Revenues by Province, 1978
(percent)

	Own-source Revenue				Transfers			Total Revenue per capita
	Taxes	Grants-in-lieu	Other	Sub-total	General Purpose	Specific Purpose	Sub-total	$
Newfoundland	42.3	2.6	12.9	57.8	6.9	35.3	42.2	182
Prince Edward Island	7.9	–	6.8	14.7	2.8	82.5	85.3	585
Nova Scotia	27.4	2.9	9.7	40.0	10.5	49.5	60.0	738
New Brunswick	36.6	–	17.6	54.2	31.7	14.1	45.8	224
Quebec	33.4	2.4	9.5	45.3	8.1	46.6	54.7	938
Ontario	40.6	2.0	11.9	54.5	5.5	40.0	45.5	989
Manitoba	42.9	4.8	12.6	60.3	2.0	37.7	39.7	892
Saskatchewan	35.1	1.4	14.5	51.0	5.0	44.0	49.0	952
Alberta	29.7	1.3	18.8	49.8	3.1	47.1	50.2	1191
British Columbia	50.9	1.3	14.6	66.8	5.6	27.6	33.2	847
Total	37.8	2.1	12.4	52.3	6.1	41.6	47.7	917*

SOURCE: Statistics Canada, *Local Government Finance 1978.*

NOTE: Percentages may not add up to subtotals because of rounding.

* Includes Yukon and Northwest Territories.

TABLE 5-3

Distribution of General Local Revenues, Selected Cities, 1977
(percent)

	Own-source Revenue				Transfers			Total Revenue per capita
	Taxes	Grants-in-lieu	Other	Sub-total	General Purpose	Specific Purpose	Sub-total	$
Montreal	37.6	2.0	11.9	51.6	9.8	38.6	48.4	991
Quebec	33.5	2.8	11.4	47.7	11.4	40.9	52.3	854
Hamilton-Wentworth	41.2	1.1	9.2	51.5	5.4	43.1	48.5	1,004
Ottawa-Carleton	39.9	7.0	8.9	55.8	4.5	39.7	44.2	1,106
Toronto	53.6	2.4	9.0	65.1	4.3	30.7	34.9	1,017
Winnipeg	50.0	5.1	12.6	67.7	2.6	29.7	32.3	844
Calgary	31.3	1.7	18.6	51.5	2.5	46.0	48.5	1,126
Edmonton	32.5	2.2	19.7	54.4	2.3	43.3	45.6	1,135
Vancouver	55.4	1.5	13.1	70.0	5.8	24.2	30.0	830

SOURCE: Statistics Canada *Local Government Finance 1977*.

NOTE: Percentages may not add up to subtotals.

Columbia, property taxes made up over one-half of all local government revenues. "Other" own-source revenues, mainly user charges, account for 12.4 percent of total local government revenues on average, with the proportion varying from a low of 6.8 percent in Prince Edward Island to a high of 18.8 percent in Alberta.[1]

With the exception of New Brunswick, specific-purpose transfers constitute a much larger proportion of total revenues than do general-purpose transfers.[2] For the country as a whole, specific-purpose transfers make up 41.6 percent of total local revenues compared to only 6.1 percent for general-purpose transfers. Specific-purpose transfers account for more than one-half of all local revenues in one province (Prince Edward Island) and close to one half in four other provinces (Nova Scotia, Quebec, Saskatchewan, and Alberta). The significant provincial role in local expenditure responsibilities noted in chapter 4 is thus verified to some extent by the proliferation of specific-purpose transfers, where the donor exercises substantial control over how the funds are spent. This point is discussed further in chapter 7.

Finally, Table 5–3 provides a breakdown of local revenues for the nine largest Canadian cities for 1977. With the exception of Quebec City, revenues from own sources made up the largest part of total local revenues, accounting for as much as 70 percent of local revenues in Vancouver, 68 percent in Winnipeg, and 65 percent in Toronto. Property taxes alone accounted for at least one-half of total local revenues in Toronto, Winnipeg, and Vancouver. Other own-source revenues (mainly user charges) are also larger than the average for all cities in most of the large cities, the exceptions being the three Ontario cities. The big cities thus rely to a greater extent on own-source revenues than do smaller cities.

THE PROPERTY TAX

No tax in Canada has been more vilified than the property tax. It has been called inherently regressive, inelastic, and an inadequate generator of municipal revenues. It has been labelled "unfair" because it is unrelated to ability to pay, "unrealistic" because it is unrelated to benefits, and "unsuitable" because it supports services unrelated to property. Its effects on housing, land use, and urban development have been castigated; the determination of its base has always been controversial because value, unlike income or sales price, is a matter of opinion, not definition; and its political unpopularity has long been acknowledged by all.

In these circumstances, it is perhaps not surprising that one of the most striking features of Canadian municipal finance in recent years has been a decline in the relative importance of property taxes as a source of revenue to finance municipal services, including education. In 1960, for example, property taxes provided two-thirds of the total revenue of Canadian municipalities; by 1977, this proportion had fallen to one-third. A similar decline is visible from almost any point of view. As a percentage of household income, for example, total property taxes in Ontario in 1970 were 3.2 percent; by 1978, this percentage was down to 2.7 percent — an increase after a low of 2.4 percent in 1974 and 1975. Although the absolute number of dollars paid in property taxes of course rose over this period, inflation and growth in real income was such that the *relative* importance of property taxes fell. Indeed, in terms of *absolute* constant dollars, per capita residential property taxes in Ontario *fell* 13 percent from 1969 to 1978.[3] Similar trends occurred also in other parts of the country.

Contrary to popular impressions, from the early 1960s until at least the mid-1970s property taxes in Canada declined in importance. Since then, however, property taxes seem again to be on the rise, albeit slowly, largely because the willingness of provincial governments to increase transfers to municipalities — in effect to finance property tax reductions (or prevent increases) — has evaporated with the squeeze on provincial revenues as a result of the economic slowdown since the late 1970s. Although concern about property taxes has never really died down, there is a little more reason for such concern now, since it appears likely that this revenue source will be drawn on more heavily in the future.

The figures mentioned above relate to *total* property taxes. Most of the public concern with property taxes, however, is focused on *residential* taxes. In a way this is hard to understand because property taxes in Canada generally discriminate in favor of residential property. In Ontario, for instance, residential property is normally assessed at a lower percentage of market value than is nonresidential property. There are, of course, wide variations within both broad categories. Moreover, residential property is subject to lower tax rates, whereas business property is subject to an additional "business tax" on the same property valuation. The net result is that the average effective tax rate on business property, at least in Ontario, is probably considerably higher than that on residential property. Nevertheless, it is changes in the residential property tax that give rise to the greatest political problems.

The obvious political reasons for levying heavier taxes on nonresidential property are supported by the greater ease of "exporting" such taxes to nonresidents, in their capacities either as owners of the taxed premises or consumers of the goods or services produced therein. In other terms, however, such "exported" taxes may be considered so undesirable that it has recently been suggested by Ballentine and Thirsk (1980) that local governments should be forbidden to tax nonresidential property at all.

Basically, the argument is that taxing nonresidential property facilitates tax exporting, thus breaching an important general principle of local finance, namely, that — in the absence of demonstrated benefit spillovers (see chapter 3) — local taxes should be paid by local residents. Ballentine and Thirsk (1980) estimate that the average rate of "exporting" nonresidential property taxes in some 29 Canadian municipalities for which data were available is 56 percent. That is, over half the total taxes levied on nonresidential property are not paid by local residents at all — but by people living in other, often poorer, communities that receive little or no benefits from the services financed by these taxes.[4] In addition to the dubious ethical merit of the nonresidential property tax, as a tax on capital it distorts the allocation of capital in the private sector, and as a relatively painless method of finance it tends to induce inefficient additional local expenditure — to the benefit, of course, of local residents who may not be willing to bear the cost of such expenditure themselves but are naturally not reluctant to reap the benefits, but to society's loss.

Local politicians would doubtless be unwilling to give up such a painless and productive revenue source — nonresidential property taxes probably account for about half of all property taxes on average and thus finance about 25 percent of all local expenditures — but there certainly seems good reason for the "provincialization" of at least this part of the property tax. This point is discussed further in chapter 6, where an additional argument regarding educational finance that points to the same solution is adduced. Until arguments such as these work their way from the academic literature into popular discussion, however, it seems likely that discussion will continue to focus on the alleged evils of residential taxes, ignoring the probably greater evils of nonresidential taxes. Partly for this reason, the remainder of the present discussion will focus on the residential part of the property tax.

Who Pays the Tax?

In recent years there has been substantial controversy on the question of who pays residential property taxes. Broadly speaking, there are two views of this issue, the "traditional view" and the "new view."[5] The traditional approach to the incidence of the property tax considers the tax as being divided, in effect, into two principal components, the tax on land and the tax on improvements, by which is meant mainly structures. As land is assumed to be in fixed supply, it follows from elementary economic analysis that the part of the tax assumed to fall on land must be borne by landowners alone; they cannot shift the burden to others through altering the quantity of land supplied.

Because the supply of structures can be altered through investment decisions, however, that portion of the property tax that is assumed to fall on structures may be shifted forward to the consumers of the services provided by structures. If the supply of structures is assumed to be perfectly elastic in the long run, that is, any amount will be supplied at the given rate of return, *all* of the tax on structures can thus be shifted forward to tenants for rented residential property, and to the consumers of the goods and services produced by commerce and industry for nonresidential property. Similarly, for owner-occupied residences, the entire tax on structures is in these circumstances borne by the owners in proportion to their imputed housing expenditures.

In reality, both tenets of the traditional theory — that the supply of land is completely inelastic, while the supply of improvements is completely elastic, or the demand completely inelastic — are open to question, particularly from the point of view of any particular taxing jurisdiction; not only can new land be created through landfill operations, for example, but municipal boundaries can be altered (Polinsky and Rubinfeld 1974; Aaron 1975, pp. 40–41).[6]

If the supply of land is *not* fixed, taxes on land will tend to affect the quantity of land supplied, which means that these taxes may be shifted to other factors of production or to consumers. Heavier land taxes in an urban area surrounded by undeveloped farmland, for example, may reduce the supply of land brought into urban use, thus raising housing prices and affecting wages and profits as well as rents.

If the supply of land *is* fixed, however, the traditional theory suggests that present landowners bear only those increases in land taxes that have been imposed since they obtained the property. All earlier taxes on land were wholly or partly, depending on a number of factors, *capitalized*, that is, resulted in a reduction of the selling price of the land at the time they were imposed; these taxes were therefore borne for all time by the previous owners, since the present owners paid sufficiently less for the taxed property to ensure that they received a normal rate of return after paying the property tax. As mentioned in chapter 3, there have been a number of capable empirical studies of property tax capitalization in recent years, some of which confirm the existence of this phenomenon, at least in part.[7] Since a capitalized tax in effect does not exist so far as present income recipients are concerned, it cannot really be shifted; exactly what is meant by the "incidence" of such a tax is therefore somewhat obscure. To the extent that past land taxes have been capitalized, current landowners can, however, be said to bear the tax in the important sense that they would be gainers if it were removed.

Turning to that part of the property tax that is assumed to fall on structures in the classical approach, the traditional assumption of a completely elastic supply of structures is of course a long-run assumption. If this part of the tax is to be fully shifted forward in the short run, it must be because the demand for the services provided by structures is completely inelastic.[8] Although this assumption is apparently often made, particularly with respect to low-income housing, it too appears to be somewhat exaggerated from the perspective of any particular taxing jurisdiction. Some poor people can, and do, move to other areas every day — and this is even truer of less-poor people. In view of the high mobility of the population throughout the country in general and within urban areas in particular, a completely inelastic demand for housing in any jurisdiction would appear to be at most a passing phenomenon.

A major problem with the conventional approach to the incidence of the property tax is that the critical dependence of the results of the analysis on the specifics of the local situation has been neglected in favor of sweeping assertions based, at best, on casual and limited observation. If there is one thing that the traditional theory makes clear, for example, it is that the short-run incidence of a property tax increase on low-rental housing in Toronto is almost certain to be different from the incidence of a similar increase on low-income, owner-occupied, single-family residences in, say, Winnipeg or Saint John. Yet the usual analysis of property tax incidence lumps the two together and makes the same extreme elasticity assumptions about both.

These defects in application, however, should not obscure the fact that the traditional theory, provided the conditions of the relevant markets are correctly specified, offers a suitable guide to policy-makers with respect to the impact on the price of housing services of *changes* in *local* taxes in the short run. What is primarily required to reap full benefits from the theory is better knowledge of local housing markets. The incidence of a marginal change in a local tax over the long run may also be analyzed within this framework, provided that the relevant market functions over time are properly specified — a task that becomes more complex as the time period lengthens, owing to the increasing implausibility of the assumption common to all such analysis that other things remain equal. A general equilibrium approach therefore becomes increasingly necessary as the years go by.[9]

In addition, municipal tax-rate changes are determined to a substantial extent by provincial policies, so that if one municipality raises its rates, others are likely doing the same thing. Even more broadly, provincial policies respond to national trends, and national trends reflect the workings of the continental, and even worldwide economy. The result is that a given increase in the tax rate in one municipality is often matched by similar increases in a much broader area — the metropolitan area, the province, the country, or North America as a whole. In these circumstances, the straightforward traditional approach ceases to be useful because it can no longer be assumed that, for example, real income and all other prices, including factor prices, remain unchanged. A general equilibrium approach is then needed to determine even the short-run incidence of a general tax change; in recent years such an approach has been applied to the property tax under the name of the "new view" of property tax incidence.

In a sense, the traditional view of the incidence of the property tax is that those who pay the tax to the government, the owners of property, do not, except for owner-occupiers, in fact "pay" the tax; rather, they shift the burden onto tenants and consumers. Oddly enough, the new view of property tax incidence is that property owners *do* pay the tax — not just the owners of the *taxed* property, however, but *all* property owners. The key factor underlying this change in result is a change in the perspective from which the problem is viewed. The traditional view deals, in effect, with the incidence of the tax in a particular locality; the new view, on the other hand, focuses on the incidence of the tax in the country as a whole. It is not too surprising that when the perspective is thus changed, something different is seen.

The initial assumption in this "new" approach is that the property tax can in the first instance be viewed as being imposed at a uniform rate on all forms of property.[10] If the total supply of land and capital is fixed, and certain other rather stringent conditions are met, the burden of such a tax must be borne in proportion to the ownership of capital for, in essence, the same reason that a land tax is borne by landowners in the traditional analysis. The tax will have no effects on the price of housing or of other goods; all it will do is lower the profits and rents of capitalists and landowners. Since capital ownership is generally considered to be more highly concentrated than income, the incidence of such a tax in terms of total income will be progressive. Despite various qualifications and modifications noted in Bird (1976b), the essence of the new view is thus that the property tax may, on a nationwide basis, be considered initially to be a capital tax, affecting the rate of return on all capital — and that it is therefore progressive in its incidence.

As with the traditional view, when properly formulated there is no doubt that the conclusions of the new view follow logically from its premises. What matters then is, first, whether these premises accord with Canadian realities and, second, whether the questions answered by the new view are those that are being asked. The answers to both points, developed below, suggest that the applicability of the new view to the relevant policy questions about residential property tax in Canada appears to be rather limited — but not nonexistent.

A principal difference between the old view and the new view concerns the elasticity of capital supply; the old view assumes implicitly that the supply of capital is perfectly inelastic, while the new view assumes explicitly that it is perfectly inelastic. It was argued above that the traditional argument might be right in some circumstances for a particular locality. The unmodified new view, that the property tax basically falls on capital owners, seems, however, to be clearly wrong even for Canada as a whole, largely because Canada is, relative to the United States, an economically small country, and one that is very open. In particular, capital is highly mobile across the border, which means that the rate of return on capital in Canada is probably set in a fundamental way by that in the United States.

On the basis of some very slim evidence, it may be hypothesized that the average effective rate of property taxation in Canada is probably less than that in the United States.[11] If the average level of the tax is in fact less in Canada *and* the rate of return on capital is, in effect, set in the United States, then in theory capital should flow into Canada until the before-tax rate of return in Canada rises sufficiently to offset the tax differential. In short, because the United States tax is higher, Canada ends up with a larger capital stock and hence higher real wages. In this sense, then, the basic average property tax may well be progressive in its overall impact on the distribution of income in Canada — but it is the fact that the Canadian tax is lower than the United States tax and not the Canadian tax itself that has this effect.

To see this, consider what would happen if the United States tax were increased; Canadian labor would become still better off. But if the *Canadian* tax were increased while the United States tax, and the rate of return on capital, were held constant, a significant part of the additional tax burden would fall on Canadian labor. For example, if as a result of the current pressures on provincial finances, grants to municipalities were cut and the effective rates of the property tax increased in Canada, the distributive impact of the increase, even on the purest new view, would appear to be basically regressive, unless rates rose simultaneously in the United States.

These effects may well be accentuated if, in addition, the effect of the average level of property tax in North America as a whole were also to reduce the level of saving. If the property tax results in a fall in saving, the capital stock will of course fall, and the tax burden will tend in the long run (which may be *very* long) to be shifted in part to less elastic factors such as labor and land (Feldstein 1974). To the extent the tax is shifted to labor, Canadian workers might then suffer a double blow. It is very difficult to assess the importance of this point, however, because the scanty available evidence on the impact of changes in the rate of return on *total* saving may best be described as inconclusive (McLure 1980). In any case, in principle, any negative effect of a particular tax measure on saving can be offset by other fiscal and monetary policies, if desired.

Similar adjustments in capital stock between industries and jurisdictions may of course take place *within* Canada. Aaron suggests that on balance the effects of such shifts are likely to be progressive in the United States, because higher tax rates tend to occur in jurisdictions with higher income levels (Aaron 1975, p. 45). If this is the case, the basic progressivity of the property tax, owing to its nature as a tax on capital, may be enhanced. On the other hand, it may well be that higher rates tend to occur in lower-income areas, in which case the "excise effects" will be regressive.

In Canada, however, the provincial role in the property tax field is much bigger than is the role of the states in the United States. Not only is the tax now basically provincial in New Brunswick, Prince Edward Island, and, with respect to assessment, in Ontario and Nova Scotia, but local tax rates are at least partly determined by provincial grant levels, which tend in turn to be distributed in part to offset inequalities in the local tax base. In short, interprovincial tax differentials in Canada appear to be smaller than those in the United States.[12] Since most provinces are bigger than most states in relative size, and interprovincial differences are in turn offset slightly by federal equalization of school taxes, it seems possible that variations in effective property tax rates within Canada as a whole may well be less than those in the United States, which means that such interjurisdictional adjustments in terms of the movement of reproducible capital would be less important.

Many other qualifications similarly reduce the level of confidence one has in the unadorned new view — without, however, in any way restoring the confidence lost in the simple traditional view as a guide to the total incidence of the property tax in Canada as a whole. The imperfectly competitive markets that pervade the real world, for example, have led some to argue that landlords will use tax increases as an excuse for raising rents, so that there is a short-run shifting of the property tax that takes place even before the capital and excise tax effects come into play (Musgrave 1974). Common as it is, however, the assumption that landlords can and do fully shift forward *all* property tax increases to tenants seems rather implausible as a generalization. The property tax is proportional not to rent but to value, and rent-value ratios are not constant for all values (Peterson 1972). Since the proportion of tax included in rent therefore varies from property to property, even collusive landlords not previously exercising their full market power appear unlikely to be able to shift it uniformly.

The advent of rent control in many Canadian cities has, of course, made such forward shifting much easier than before; as always, cartel-like behavior is easier to sustain when supported by government than when opposed by it. Nevertheless, investigations of the land and housing markets in Toronto, for example, do not suggest that market conditions are as conducive to shifting as is commonly asserted.[13] There may well be some short-run shifting in some segments of the market, but it is hard to see grounds for assuming this shifting to be pervasive and complete, at least prior to rent control. Finally, as is often true in economic policy, the variations from the class mean may well be greater than those between means, so that the policy significance of variations between income classes is open to considerable doubt.[14]

Even this brief discussion makes it clear that more information is needed on many points before the applicability or inapplicability of the new view of the property tax in Canada can be determined with much confidence: the elasticities of substitution in production and consumption, the elasticities of supply and demand for capital, the mobility of factors, factor intensities, the degree of competition, the initial tax structure and its income effects, etcetera. Furthermore, the above discussion suggests clearly that there is no single answer to the question, "Who pays the property tax?" Rather, there will be many answers, depending on the sizes of the parameters listed above, and the time and geographical framework within which the question is asked.

Nevertheless, it is probably safe to conclude that the conventional view almost certainly overstates the regressivity of the property tax, in part because it considers only the "uses-of-income" side, while ignoring the effects on the sources of income; and in part because it takes too extreme a position on the relevant elasticities. While this ancient levy is certainly not the best of all possible taxes, it is, it now seems, not necessarily the hopeless fiscal villain it has sometimes been made out to be.

It is particularly important to specify clearly the questions that one is concerned with when considering the incidence of the property tax. If one's major concern is with a particular tax change in a particular city, something much like the modified traditional view of incidence may well be close to the truth; but if one's major concern is with the differential incidence of property taxes in general, then the modified new view is likely to be closer.[15] In either case, close attention will have to be paid to far more variables and specific conditions than in any existing Canadian studies of property tax incidence.

No matter what one thinks of the incidence of the property tax in theory, however, the way in which the tax is actually administered remains vitally important, not only to the actual incidence of the tax, but also to how citizens *perceive* the tax, and consequently to how they react to proposals to change its role in the fiscal system.[16] A tax that is frequently reassessed on a uniform, province-wide basis, as so many reports have urged, would be a quite different tax from the present nonuniform, infrequently altered, often locally administered levy found in most parts of Canada. Whether it would be a *better* tax, however, is perhaps more open to discussion.[17]

One must not make the mistake of considering the property tax in isolation. In addition to such personal income tax offsets to property taxes as the nontaxation of the imputed income on equity in owner-occupied houses and the exemption of principal residences from capital gains tax,[18] on the whole the corporate income tax burdens the housing sector less than most other parts of the economy. Just as demand is channeled into housing through the effects of the structure of the income tax, so, for this reason, is some supply of capital. When the effects of sales taxes on building materials but not on housing services, and special tax incentives such as those for the construction of rental property are considered, the net effect of the tax system — let alone of other government activities in the housing field — on housing markets is quite unclear.

Whether or not the existing property tax affects low-income groups adversely, several provinces have introduced various forms of income tax credits and direct grants allegedly intended to offset the regressive effect of property taxes on low-income groups. The major beneficiaries of these measures have been elderly homeowners. In most cases, such homeowners do not have mortgages and would not therefore benefit from such provisions as the mortgage interest deduction proposed in 1979 by the Conservative government — a provision that would have benefited most young homeowners with mortgages, particularly those with larger incomes.

While the effects of measures such as these on income distribution and housing demand are very difficult to analyze, on the whole a fair conclusion is probably that none of these measures are likely to have much effect.[19] Viewed as a part of the total tax system, for example, property tax relief distributes benefits in accordance with people's holdings of a certain form of wealth (residential property) rather than in accordance with their needs measured in any sense that seems normatively acceptable. Similarly, the effect of these measures on housing markets is minute because for most people they have no apparent effect on the price of housing. It is hard to avoid the conclusion that much of the concern with the distributional effect of taxes, particularly local taxes, has been misdirected in recent years.

Assessment System

As noted above, any analysis of the property tax must obviously take into account how the tax is actually administered.[20] Unfortunately, there are few published data in Canada on variations by type of property in the relation between assessed values and market values (the assessment-sales ratio). The most thorough study of this question still appears to be that in the Smith Report on data for 22 Ontario municipalities, including Metro Toronto, in the early 1960s.[21] This study found: (1) wide variations in the assessment-sales ratio within particular municipalities, (2) significant variations between municipalities, (3) generally higher ratios for apartments, and (4) generally lower ratios on land than on buildings. In short, there was considerable evidence of discrimination in prevailing assessing practice against apartments and in favor of single-family residences, as well as substantial undervaluation of land in all classes of property. Although long suspected, these aspects of the assessment system had not previously been documented in detail, since Ontario, unlike many United States jurisdictions, but like most other provinces, does not publish the results of any assessment-sales ratio studies that may or may not be carried out. An earlier study by Clayton (1966) had also suggested a possible tendency to over-assess lower-valued homes relative to higher-valued homes.

The most detailed published study of assessment patterns since the Smith report was carried out in what is now the Region of Peel in 1970, when a new assessment was carried out in the then Town of Mississauga.

This study found that market-value assessment resulted in a marked shift of the tax base to residential properties. Within the residential sector, single-family houses, especially older houses with substantial land, were found to be especially undervalued (Bureau of Municipal Research 1970). Land values in this area had of course grown sharply in the 1960s, and have continued to do so since.

The scanty evidence available thus suggests that Ontario assessing practice — and probably that elsewhere — has long implicitly discriminated in favor of residential property. The apparent pattern of discrimination may be sketched along the following lines. First, residential property is underassessed relative to commercial and industrial realty. Second, apartment buildings are overassessed relative to single-family houses. Third, land values are underassessed everywhere. Fourth, newer buildings are overassessed relative to older ones. Fifth, low-value, rented residential units, whether apartments or not, are probably overassessed relative to high-value units.

To illustrate this pattern of assessment discrimination, compare two buildings of equal market value in Metropolitan Toronto, located in, say, the City of Toronto and the neighboring Borough of Scarborough. The latter is probably taxed more heavily, assuming the nominal tax rates and the levels of service received are the same, because it is almost certainly newer. If the city structure is rented, however, and the Scarborough one is owner-occupied — also a likely situation — one assessment bias may be offset by another, and the result is unclear. New, low-rent structures in Toronto, if such existed, would of course be doubly adversely affected by these assessment practices. If one assumes, however, that low-income people in the suburbs tend to live in owner-occupied houses and in the city in rental properties, as may be true, the various assessment biases may tend to be offsetting in terms of their effects on the incidence of the property tax by income classes.

More generally, all residents of single-family houses, and particularly those in older houses with larger land areas, have probably long been favored by assessing practice in Ontario, as in most jurisdictions. Any such persistent pattern of discriminatory assessments must grow out of and be maintained by political pressures and the operation of the political process. This proposition is particularly easy to sustain in Ontario because of the history of the split-mill rate, in which the residential tax rate is lower than the commercial/industrial tax rate, and the unhappy fate of the recent proposals for revising the tax system before introducing market-value assessment.[22]

A final important characteristic of the Canadian assessment system that deserves mention is its secrecy. This secrecy gives rise to difficulties for ordinary homeowners contemplating an appeal against the valuation of their property. Only those with the resources to conduct their own comparative appraisal studies have much chance of arguing successfully with the assessor unless he has gotten some obvious physical fact wrong. The secrecy of assessment procedures thus tends to make the appeals procedure, to some extent, the recourse of the rich, which in turn suggests that the net effect of appeals may be to make the impact of the property tax more regressive than it would otherwise be.

More importantly, the perceived and actual difficulty of the formal appeal procedure for ordinary taxpayers is probably one factor leading to considerable use of other, more informal means of "tax protesting" through publicity and political contacts both at the local and, especially in recent years, the provincial level. This use of "voice" (see chapter 4) may be generated in the first place in response to perceived inequities and administrative arbitrariness affecting an individual. In the absence of information on the relative fairness with which the person is being treated, however, it is likely to take the form of general complaints about the whole institution of property taxation such as those so often heard in recent years.

An Evaluation

Despite its defects and the uncertainty about its incidence, the residential property tax on the whole appears to be about as fair and efficient a tax as can be administered at the local level. The defects of the tax are, at least in principle, largely correctable — for example, through provincial assessment. And in many cases the defects are exaggerated in the popular mind. Its regressivity, for example, may well be offset by the distributive effects of the services it finances, whether such services are provided "to property" or "to people."

In this connection, however, it perhaps deserves emphasis that the residential property tax can only very loosely be considered a benefit tax. To the extent that public services provided to property (roads, sewers, etcetera) enhance the value of that property and are not fully paid for through user charges, they result in higher property taxes. Similarly, if less directly, higher levels of educational services, financed in part through property taxes, may make a municipality a more desirable place to live, even for those without current school-age children, and can thus be justified to some extent on benefit grounds. This point, however, is not too important in Canada owing to the dominant provincial role in educational finance (see chapter 6).

It is clear that much of the property tax — especially that large portion paid by nonresidential property, and often exported to other jurisdictions — cannot easily be justified on these benefit grounds. Indeed, even the "property-related" services now financed through property taxes might in some instances be more fairly and efficiently financed through user charges, as discussed in chapter 6. The defence of property taxation in the end must thus rest only weakly on its "benefit" character.

An alternative defence — mentioned earlier in chapter 2 — in effect adopts a different model of what an ideal urban revenue system should be, a conception closer to that implicit in the "public choice" perspective described in chapter 3. Under this approach — which Break (1980) calls the "restraining-rules-and-process" model — the residential property tax should play a central role in local finance precisely because it enables taxpayers to identify clearly, in terms of personal consequences, the impact of public-sector expenditure decisions. In these circumstances, it is argued, local governments are most unlikely to engage in expenditures that are not perceived by their taxpayers to be at least as beneficial as the pain induced by the taxes required to pay for them.

Even those who view the urban revenue system in terms of neither a "benefit" nor a "process" model but of a less appropriate "ability-to-pay" model,[23] despite their avowed distaste for the property tax, have generally found it to be too valuable a source of local revenue for local purposes, and thus a bulwark of local autonomy, to make any drastic changes seem advisable. The property tax has thereby survived a storm of official and unofficial abuse for decades. Indeed, it has remained the most important single source of local revenues under local control throughout Canada, and hence a crucial element in the governmental structure of this country. Its very persistence in the face of such criticism suggests that it must have some virtues, hidden though they might be.

Influenced by the prevailing negative attitude toward the tax, however, all provincial governments have in recent years taken measures to alleviate what are generally considered to be its major defects, particularly its regressivity. These measures have taken three principal forms: first, relief of pressure on the tax by provincial assumption of local functions and by increased provincial transfers to municipalities; second, removal of the apparent regressivity of the tax through such devices as split-mill rates — with higher rates, most inappropriately, levied on nonresidential property — exemptions, and property tax credits; and, third, rectification of some of its administrative deficiencies through such measures as provincial takeover of all or part of the assessment function, assessment at full market value, and more frequent reassessment. Several provinces — notably, Ontario, New Brunswick, Prince Edward Island, and, most recently, Nova Scotia — have taken considerable steps in all these directions, and all provinces have taken at least some such action.

As noted above, from an economic point of view, taxes on residential property should clearly be higher than taxes on nonresidential property on both benefit and equity grounds, as well as in terms of economic efficiency. For political reasons, however, what seems likely to continue to happen in the future is exactly the opposite, with taxes on nonresidential property continuing to rise more quickly than those on residences. Perhaps the most desirable change that could be made in the property tax would be to move the taxation of nonresidential property, if it is to continue to exist at all, up to the provincial level, thereby avoiding many of the evils of local tax competition that ensue when the tax is at the municipal level. The next chapter suggests a means of combining this desirable reform with a similar reform in the financing of the educational system. The same chapter also argues that user charges should become a much more important source of local revenue than is now the case. To the extent that this happens, the importance of the residential property tax — considered as a surrogate user charge for various services provided by the municipality — might also decline as a source of municipal revenues.

There would still remain, however, a need for a general local revenue source, which the residential property tax could usefully satisfy. Even if in the long run, one could perhaps envisage a decline in the role of local property taxes, with education, for example, being financed more by upper levels of government and local services by user charges, in the short run, the opposite — an increased demand on local property tax revenues — seems a more likely prospect.

To conclude, the property tax has been with us for many years. Because of the desirability of having some independent local taxes, and because of administrative constraints on other revenue sources, it is likely to be with us for many more years. Contrary to what is sometimes implied, this is not a disaster. On the whole, the property tax is not nearly as bad a fiscal instrument as it has sometimes been painted. In an ideal system its role would no doubt be smaller, but it is not likely ever to disappear.

ALTERNATIVE SOURCES OF FINANCE

This last section considers briefly the possibility of alternative changes in urban revenues, first in property-related levies, and then by moving to reliance on income and sales taxes.

Another approach to property tax reform, which offers the additional benefit of removing the disincentive to improve property inherent in the present or the market-value system, is to move to a "land value" basis, levying taxes only on the value of the site and not on the buildings occupying that site. This proposal is, as experience in various countries has shown, quite workable (see Holland, 1970); it also has such potential advantages as encouraging better land use and reducing urban sprawl (see Becker 1969). Nonetheless, it is not likely to prove very popular in Canada. While most would doubtless applaud substantial increases in taxes on vacant land, older, single-family homes in central areas would — just as under the market-value system—generally suffer very large tax increases under a site-value tax, thereby in all probability leading to the same political protests that have stymied most recent attempts at property tax reform.[24]

A bolder and more experimental approach might be to take at their word all those who talk about the property tax as though it were payment for municipal services and move the tax closer to a true benefit basis. As noted in chapter 6, there are indeed very considerable advantages, and few disadvantages, to be gained by charging more directly for many more municipal services. It may well be that a thoroughgoing revamping of the property tax along benefit lines would form a desirable part of a move in this direction. As Vickrey (1963) noted, however, few benefit-related charges would vary with the value of either land or buildings; instead, such factors as land area and front footage seem more likely to provide the best basis for a benefit-related property tax. The local tax might still be called a "property tax," but in such a system it would really be more a bundle of property-related user charges than a levy related in any simple way to the gross value of real property. Bossons (1981) has, for example, put forth a detailed proposal for reform of the Ontario property tax that may be interpreted along these lines. The resulting redistribution of burdens among taxpayers, though probably not identical to the shifts that would occur with market-value assessment, would be, in all likelihood, as difficult to sell politically as market-value assessment itself. Like land-value taxation, benefit-based property taxation may be an idea whose time has not yet come.

Special Assessments and Lot Levies

Another group of property-related levies that have received increasing attention in recent years, especially in rapidly growing cities, are lot levies, subdivision exactments, and similar devices intended to defray the cost of certain public-sector capital outlays attributable to the creation of new housing subdivisions.[25] More generally, it can be argued that more use should be made of the related system called "special assessments" or local-improvement taxes to finance public works undertaken in other areas as well.

Many public works directly increase the value of the properties that they serve, thereby providing a financial benefit to the property owners. Since these owners benefit from the improvements through no efforts of their own, it seems appropriate to charge them for the costs. There are several ways this can be done. One approach is to require developers to provide certain services, such as water, sewers, and parks, to municipal standards before they are permitted by the municipality to develop and sell lots. A second possibility is a subdivision agreement between the developer and the municipality in which the developer pays a "lot levy" to the municipality to provide certain services. A third option is to have the municipality provide the services and then charge the property owners through special assessments. A fourth possibility is to have the developer provide all services internal to the subdivision and have the municipality charge a lot levy for off-site services. Finally, the municipality can provide all or part of the services and finance them from such general revenue sources as the property tax.

Traditionally, special assessments under such names as local-improvement taxes or capital levies have been employed in a variety of ways in Canadian municipalities. In Ontario, for example, 50 to 100 percent of the capital cost of such local improvements as sidewalks and sewers have been recovered by special assessments, usually in the form of a front-footage charge on owners whose properties abutted the work in question.[26] In no case have such charges produced much revenue, however. The situation in other provinces seems equally complex and inconsistent, being based more on custom than on reason.

For the most part, special assessments in Canada have been confined to relatively minor public works in existing neighborhoods; perhaps the major exception has been the extension of sewer systems to already built-up fringe areas. The growing need in some older cities to finance the reconstruction of decaying infrastructure provides ample reason for reconsideration and rationalization of these policies in the future. Of more immediate concern, however, has been the continuing need to create new infrastructure to accommodate residential and industrial expansion. For the most part, such capital works have been financed in Ontario through "lot levies," or cash imposts on developers of new subdivisions that are intended to cover the costs of providing water, sewers, roads, street lights, and so on.

A recent study of the structure of lot levies in a group of contiguous regional municipalities surrounding Toronto, where most new housing in Ontario has been located in recent years, found that all of the 24 local municipalities surveyed charge developers of single-family, detached houses levies ranging from $750 per lot to $3,700 (Amborski 1980). In addition, the four regional municipalities in the area — which are responsible, for example, for providing water service — also charge levies ranging from $250 to $2,430. The total lot levy charged in 1979 in these municipalities ranged from a low of $2,000 to a high of $4,969. Some municipalities apply uniform levies to all new residential developments, while others differentiate by housing type, and some go as far as differentiating by the number of bedrooms. In some instances, the levies charged were increased annually or semiannually in accordance with some price index (usually a construction-cost index).

Where the pricing mechanism used as the basis of lot levies is explicitly stated, it is usually some form of average-cost pricing, which generally means average per capita costs multiplied by the average number of persons per type of unit. Efforts to use any form of marginal-cost pricing have been limited. Those municipalities that differentiate lot levies according to housing type in effect try to recognize the incremental costs of each additional person in a unit, but they still use average costs as the basis for the levy.

Some jurisdictions differentiate their levies according to what services are available. This attempt to relate the levy more closely to the benefits received is admirable but, again, average-cost pricing is used. On the whole, none of the extensive Ontario experience with lot levies appears to show any obvious influence of the enormous economics literature on the efficient pricing of public services (see chapter 6).

In analytical terms, both special assessments and lot levies may be considered to be methods of capturing anticipated "betterment" or increases in property values. Special assessments, for example, are intended to recapture the cost of such special local improvements as sidewalks fairly by allocating the cost among properties in accordance with some arbitrarily determined, presumed pattern of benefits. In reality, it is clear that since "other things" are never equal, any increases in property values consequent to an improvement can only very roughly be attributed to that improvement. It is in part for this reason that the greatest potential for special assessments perhaps lies in rapidly expanding communities, where any errors in benefit attribution would tend to be swamped by other factors. The effects of special assessments on property values depend only in part upon their accuracy as benefit taxes, however. Perhaps even more important is the question of whether the earmarked funding they provide is perceived as increasing the quantity and quality of public capital works.

Like special assessments, lot levies are imposed on select groups in a particular area. Unlike special assessments, such levies are a very recent phenomenon, having largely been created in response to the pressure on urban resources arising from rapid urbanization. As the above description of current Ontario practice suggests, it is difficult to conclude that the formulas currently used to determine such levies are either fair or efficient. This is the result not so much of the deficiencies of municipal administration as of the intractable nature of the problem. In effect, every individual subdivision proposal gives rise to different infrastructure costs and environmental effects, and therefore ideally requires an individually determined formula. To reduce uncertainty — and the influence of interdependent bargaining behavior — many municipalities have developed rough rules of thumb instead of deciding each case on its particular merits. Such rules are, of course, generally inappropriate in some respects for each particular case. When they are too obviously inappropriate — or when enough pressure is applied — most municipalities have in fact proved amenable to some negotiation.[27] The outcome of this combination of essentially arbitrary rules with the possibility of individual adjustment has often been to maximize political conflict in the process and inequity and inefficiency in the results.

The conclusion of the brief review in this section is, perhaps surprisingly, that the ancient instrument of special assessments may have more to be said for it than the new tool of lot levies, or subdivision exactments generally. Both devices have distinct merits in terms of equity and perhaps political acceptability in comparison with the property tax. Both are also inherently somewhat arbitrary and hence give rise to horizontal inequities in the form of windfall gains and losses. Lot levies create more uncertainty, however, and as often applied, shift more of the financing costs onto developers. They thus tend to block development and may affect resource allocation adversely, while special assessments have little, if any, adverse allocative effect. Moreover, since the era of rapid urban expansion appears to be almost past in most cities, devices such as lot levies, which are only applicable on the urban fringe, will inevitably fade in importance relative to the continual need to improve and replace capital works that can be financed through special assessments.

In view of the strength of the case for more use of special-assessment financing and the resistance to local property taxes, it is surprising that so little attention has been paid to this subject in North American municipalities in recent years. In particular, more explicit consideration seems needed of the case for using special assessments to cover the capital costs and user charges to cover the current costs of a wide range of urban services (see also chapter 6).

Income and Sales Taxes

The major revenue sources of governments in Canada as a whole are sales and income taxes, which together account for close to 90 percent of total taxes collected (Bird 1979, p. 31). It is not surprising, therefore, that there have frequently been suggestions that local governments too should be permitted to tap these sources, which are at present reserved for higher levels of government. This final section therefore considers briefly the case for and against municipal sales and income taxes in Canada.

In the first place, it should be noted that both these levies have existed at the local level in the past in this country and still exist in some parts of the United States. Moreover, in the case of the income tax, local governments in a number of European countries — especially Scandinavia — rely almost exclusively upon this source to finance their extensive expenditures. Either a municipal income or a municipal sales tax is therefore clearly a possible alternative or supplement to property taxes.

This is not to say, however, that either is necessarily desirable. In the case of municipal sales taxes, for example, experience in Quebec before 1964, and in the United States, suggests that the evasion problem can be serious, as well as economically distorting. Large rate differentials between neighboring communities are unlikely to be sustainable over long periods of time. Even in the case of a long-established local sales tax in such a large metropolitan area as New York City, careful analyses suggest that there are substantial economic losses as a result of sales tax differentials.[28]

An additional city "piggyback" sales tax of 1 or 2 percent on a provincial tax may have few such effects, however, and since sales to nonresidents should be exempted, it is likely to be economically or politically very distorting. Nevertheless, there appears to be little enthusiasm in any quarter for the introduction of such a levy, perhaps because sales taxes are seen to be little better than property taxes in terms of elasticity and perhaps even worse in terms of incidence. The addition of a municipal sales tax to Canada's already complex mixture of federal and provincial sales taxes thus seems unlikely in the near future.

Much more attention has been devoted to the possibility of affording local access to the lucrative and expanding income tax base.[29] As in the case of sales taxes, two quite different kinds of municipal income tax are conceivable. The first — the most common type in Europe — is to levy a local tax, like most provincial income taxes, as a proportion of the federal personal income tax.[30] The second would be a separate, locally administered income tax. Since under the second approach it would be almost impossible to tax recipients of capital income fully and fairly, in practice a separate local income tax would probably degenerate into a payroll tax — and be exported in part with commuters, who may get some but not all the benefits of the expenditures it finances. Such a tax would not accord very well with either the ability or the benefit approach to urban finance.

For this reason, the first, or "piggyback," approach — with the municipal income tax essentially a surtax on the provincial-federal tax — seems the only one worth considering. Perhaps the major obstacle to use of the income tax for this purpose is simply that this levy is already the mainstay of both the federal and provincial revenue systems. It is also unclear — as Break (1980, p. 254) notes — whether local taxpayers would themselves welcome an increased reliance on income taxes that fall clearly on local residents rather than the present mixture of residential and nonresidential property taxes. On the whole, however, if there is an acceptable alternative to the residential property tax as a source of general municipal revenue, it is likely to be some sort of local income tax surcharge.

Like the property tax, such an income tax would be visible; the criterion of political responsibility and accountability would thus be satisfied. Unlike the property tax, the incidence of such a levy would in all probability generally be considered progressive across incomes, though it would seem to be almost unrelated to benefits received from municipal expenditures. Moreover, revenues from this source would almost certainly tend to expand more quickly — or at least with less open political fuss — than in the case of the property tax. In the end, therefore, apart from the important practical problem that it is most unlikely that the provinces would give the municipalities access to income taxes anyway, whether the income tax or the property tax is considered the most suitable as the mainstay of local finance probably depends largely on which of the three "models" of urban fiscal systems discussed above dominates. The ability model points to the income tax, while the benefit and process models tend to support continued reliance on the property tax.

6 Pricing Urban Services

The rapid growth period of most Canadian cities appears to be over; some, indeed, are even losing population. Although a few cities in western Canada continue to expand rapidly, one might well think that the pressures on urban finance should have been somewhat alleviated by the slowdown of urban growth. This does not, however, appear to have happened. Indeed, the problems of urban finance seem at least as severe when population growth slows as when it accelerates. Growing cities need a capital infrastructure and resources to maintain service levels for a larger population; stagnant and declining cities need to replace old infrastructure; and both must pay relatively higher prices for the resources required to produce the service levels people have come to expect. Moreover, as noted in chapter 5, the urban fiscal problem has been considerably exacerbated in recent years by increasing taxpayer resistance to the traditional mainstay of urban public finance — the local property tax. That there is often little logical basis for this resistance does not make it any less politically important. In these circumstances, cities in Canada have become increasingly dependent on aid from higher levels of government. Indeed, as noted earlier, the decline in the relative importance of property tax revenues has been almost exactly offset by the rise in the relative importance of intergovernmental transfers.

It is striking, however, that the oft-discussed revenue pressures of recent years have not resulted in any great effort to exploit nontax revenues more heavily. The combined total of special assessments and nontax revenues rose from 12.2 percent of revenues in Canada in 1970 to only 13.3 percent in 1977. The reliance of local governments on user charges in particular, varies considerably from province to province, ranging in 1978 from less than 3 percent of total municipal revenues in Nova Scotia to 13 percent in neighboring New Brunswick.[1] In Ontario, for example, user charges accounted for 5 percent of total municipal revenues in 1978. Among the major expenditure functions for which user charges are important in Ontario are the traditional areas of water, transit, sewers, and parks and recreation. More surprisingly, perhaps, user charges are also important in some "social" areas, notably assistance for the aged, in the form of charges for room and board in homes for the aged. User charges are thus most common in financing the traditional "hard" areas of transportation and water and sewers and, to a lesser extent, a few social services.

Reliance on local user charges has probably been relatively low in Canada in part precisely because of the readiness to finance urban services through intergovernmental transfers. Increasing fiscal pressures on upper-level governments in recent years, however, make it appear unlikely that these transfers will be so generous in the future. More attention may thus be paid to the possibility of financing urban public services through "user charges" — as broadly defined here to include a range of prices, charges, and fees.[2]

User charges are thus most likely to be viewed by hard-pressed urban officials as a potential additional source of revenue. To an economist, however, the real value of user charges is to promote economic efficiency by providing information to consumers and officials, enabling them to make more efficient use of resources. In an interesting article Wilbur Thompson (1968) labeled the city "a distorted price system" and pointed out the need for more rational urban prices to ration the use of existing facilities, to guide the distribution of income, to enlarge the range of choice, and to change tastes and behavior. In a sense, the principal purpose of this chapter is to outline briefly a few ways in which more reliance on user charges might reduce the present level of urban "distortion."

THE CASE FOR PRICING

The major virtue of pricing urban public services whenever possible is to improve efficiency (see also chapter 4). The major cost of doing so is, on the one hand, that it is expensive to price and, on the other, that the distributional consequences of pricing are often thought undesirable. Any argument in favor of a policy of charging for more urban public services must therefore pay attention not only to the potential gains from pricing in terms of revenue, improved knowledge of consumer needs, and improved efficiency, but also to its limitations from the points of view of administration, politics, and distribution.

As noted in chapter 3, a principal rationale for the existence of local government is that it permits the provision of public services in a diverse variety of ways to suit individual preferences. Fiscal decentralization and the local provison of, say, elementary education services provide one of the few means we have of determining the optimal amount of such services that should be provided. The major difficulty in implementing this quasi-market approach to local finance is, of course, the readily observed fact that different areas have substantially different levels of income and wealth, and that interlocal mobility and local choice are not in fact free. Because it is generally accepted that the consumption of services such as education by individuals should not be dependent on their ability to pay, there are obviously severe difficulties in carrying this view too far. Nevertheless, for many purposes it is useful to think of local taxes, particularly the property tax, as constituting, in a sense, a kind of membership fee one pays for residing in a particular area.[3]

The important role of the property tax as a direct source of finance for local services suggests that the user charge component of local tax payments, as broadly conceived, is in reality larger than the figures cited above might suggest, particularly in the relatively homogeneous dormitory suburbs in which increasing numbers of Canadians live. Indeed, the high degree of public acceptance of the idea that there is a strong benefit element in local property taxes is indicated by the frequency with which such groups as the old, farmers, and cottagers seek relief from all or part of the property tax burden on the grounds that they receive no direct benefit from the school services that the taxes largely finance.

The extent to which local finance *should* be efficiency-oriented rather than equity-oriented is an important foundation of the arguments in the present chapter. As noted in chapter 3, the position taken here is, in brief, that redistribution for its own sake is *not* a proper function of local government, and that those local fiscal policies that are designed primarily with redistributive objectives in mind are generally both ineffective and inefficient.[4] It is therefore assumed in the remainder of this chapter that the appropriate ideal for local finance is to approximate as closely as possible to the efficient pricing of government-provided services. With regard to taxes on property, what this means is more reliance on specific-benefit financing such as special assessments and lot levies (see chapter 5), and less on the general property tax — especially the nonresidential tax — while with regard to other sources of local revenue, it obviously means more emphasis on user service charges of various sorts.

As noted earlier, local governments already earn substantial amounts from enterprises in such fields as water supply, electricity, and transportation. In many cases, these activities are legally governed separately by special-purpose bodies. A few years ago, for example, the Bureau of Municipal Research (1968) noted that there were 101 units of local government in Metropolitan Toronto, 94 of which were special-purpose bodies. The Bureau further estimated that there were over 3,200 such bodies in Ontario as a whole. While not all of these special-purpose units raised funds directly by taxing or charging, there were 13 enterprise authorities in Toronto that were essentially self-financing (Toronto Transit Commission, Toronto Harbour Commission, et cetera) and a significant number of other agencies that had some control over their own finances. Whether or not such fragmentation of authority is politically desirable or economically efficient is too broad a question to be dealt with in this book, apart from the brief discussion in chapter 4.[5] It may be noted, however, that while the appropriate domain for benefit finance at the local level is much broader than that encompassed by the usual municipal enterprises and boards, an appropriate revision of the charging policies customarily followed by these agencies should rank high among the priorities of urban fiscal reformers. Later in this chapter we shall consider briefly the case of water pricing as one example.

In sharp contrast to the general case sketched briefly above for treating local finance as an appropriate domain for the pricing principle, the Canadian urban public economy is better characterized by ". . . a general unwillingness to use the price mechanism for urban services" (Crowley and Hartwick 1972). The useful allocative role that prices can play in the urban public sector has been grossly neglected in practice. Not only have the potential virtues of prices as rationing and demand-signaling devices been neglected, but the failure to price properly also means that there has been a good deal of unplanned and implicit redistribution in kind, much of which would probably not be acceptable if it were made explicit.[6]

In addition to the distributive argument against more use of the charging principle in urban public finance, there is a classic confusion that is sometimes employed to argue against *any* levying of service charges by local government. As stated by an American municipal official, the argument goes like this: ". . . any service provided by a local government agency is in the public interest [because if it were not in the public interest it would presumably not be provided] . . . it follows that the cost of the service should be provided by the entire public." (Blum 1968, p. 102).

The problem with this argument, of course, is that it assumes urban public services are either *completely* private or *completely* public in nature. In real life, however, as noted in chapter 3, most government activities do not fall into this neat black-and-white dichotomy but are instead different shades of gray.

There are, as any public finance textbook points out at length, many reasons why services may be provided by the public sector; there are also some reasons why certain services ought, in the interest of efficiency or equity, not to be charged for directly; but there is no presumption that *all* items in the first class fall into the second class. In fact, they clearly do not, particularly in the case of local government. There is, therefore, no presumption at all that local public services should be provided free. Indeed, there is rather a presumption that they *should* be charged for, at least to some extent, if we are to have any hope of providing the right mix and amount of services in the sense of what people want and are willing to pay for.

It is not possible here to go into urban pricing practices and possibilities in all areas in detail. Instead, we shall simply provide a few illustrations of what can and should be done, drawing largely on Bird (1976a). The next few sections, therefore, discuss the pricing of recreation services, of refuse collection, and of water. The chapter concludes with a look at some rather different issues involved in the important area of education finance. These discussions are intended primarily to illustrate something of the range and variety of the pricing issue within the urban public sector rather than to be a comprehensive review of this complex area.[7]

PRICING PUBLIC RECREATION

The appropriate pricing policy for public recreational facilities is likely to become increasingly important as leisure comes to occupy a larger proportion of our time, and as more and more Canadians come to live in large urban areas where accessible parkland is expensive and cheap parks are further away.

Well over half of public recreation expenditure in Canada already takes place at the municipal level, and it is municipalities that offer the widest variety of recreation services — parks, swimming pools, arenas, playgrounds, baseball fields, soccer fields, tennis courts, bowling alleys, community centres, lawn bowling, museums, lacrosse boxes, and art galleries. The charging policy followed by towns and cities with respect to these facilities is very diverse, but a few general patterns can be perhaps detected. Most municipalities collect fees for swimming pools and ice arenas, for example, perhaps in part because of the obvious costliness of a pool or arena. On the other hand, few, if any, appear to charge for either parks or playgrounds, although fees for organized summer playgroups held in those areas are not uncommon.

There is no evidence that those municipalities that charge admission for such facilities as swimming pools, however, have any objective in mind other than recouping operating costs. For example, there is little indication of attempts to affect the use of arenas by levying different fees and rentals at different times of the day.

The common pricing feature of lower rates for children, who are more likely to use the facility at off-peak hours, may in part represent an attempt to ration through pricing, but it is not a very efficient way since the low rates apply at all times. Lower prices can also perhaps be rationalized as an investment in the physical health of children.

Few, if any, municipalities appear to employ two-part pricing, that is, to require an initial membership fee and then a small fee for each admission thereafter, as might be advisable if full costs are to be recovered.[8] Indeed, as a rule no attempt is made to recover full costs at all. In a recent discussion of swimming pool finance, for example, the following pricing principles were cited: "to give everyone from all economic backgrounds the opportunity to use these public facilities; to maintain a high level of participation; and to offset as much as possible the costs involved in the employment of special instructors and the materials used in swim classes and special activities" (Flogstad 1970). In this particular case, the pricing structure was more complex than is common in Canada, with three daily admission rates varying with age, and three-month and twelve-month passes, as well as fees for lessons, and hourly rental charges. Nevertheless, the failure even to consider the key economic functions of prices as ways of rationing access to a scarce resource, and signaling how much consumers were willing to pay for such access, is both striking and characteristic.

In principle, several specific characteristics of public recreational facilities that should affect the level and nature of recreation pricing may be identified. In the first place, it seems clear that the major output of most recreation facilities should be treated as constituting a *private* consumption good to those who use the facilities. There may be, of course, also some benefits to nonusers from knowing the facilities exist (this is sometimes called "option demand"), and perhaps from some sort of general improvement of societal health and well-being, but any such external effects would appear to be definitely secondary and minor in character. In other words, such goods are more like private than public goods (see chapter 3), therefore, charging users full costs, or close to it, would appear to make sense.

Secondly, different facilities vary considerably both in the nature of the services provided and in the extent to which complementary private expenditures on time, travel, and equipment are required in order to take advantage of them. Further, many recreation services that are provided by the public sector are also available in the private sector — tennis courts, golf courses, swimming pools, campsites, and so on.

As might be expected, the characteristics of the users of different facilities are also likely to vary substantially. In addition to the incalculable effects of personal taste, income levels obviously tend to affect the recreations pursued by different people. On the average, the income profile of people who play tennis or golf is quite different from that of those who crowd an inner-city playground or swimming pool on a hot summer weekend. The major distributional considerations affecting recreational pricing come into play only where the latter kinds of facilities are concerned. Recently, some mildly persuasive evidence suggesting that the distribution of urban recreation services may favor the poor has been put forward (Gold 1974). If so, charging for such recreation services may be undesirable, particularly if, as seems possible, urban public recreation services are an "inferior good" — that is, one the consumption of which might be expected to decrease as income and the consumption of private recreation increases.

Even with respect to such urban facilities, however, unless one assumes recreation facilities will automatically receive as high a priority in local budgets as, say, road construction — which seems unlikely — there may be reason to consider the possible advantages of pricing in signaling when to expand capacity, and providing the wherewithal to do so.[9] As always, problems arising from a basically unsatisfactory distribution of income are best dealt with directly rather than indirectly, although this is easier to say than to do. Subsidizing recreation for everyone is a poor way to help the poor.

The best case for free provision of recreation facilities is clearly the one for small urban parks, both on a distributional and administrative cost basis. However, the possibility of recapturing through special assessments (see chapter 5) some of the benefits accruing to nearby property owners, in addition to the possible partial recapture through the property tax, might warrant attention even in this instance. Distributional considerations actually *support* full-cost pricing for facilities that are used mainly by those who can afford to travel to them and spend the time and money to learn to use them. Furthermore, in some instances those users may be more than willing to pay fees to improve the quality of the facility, whether it be tennis courts or a golf course.

A third characteristic of many public recreational facilities is that they are substantially underutilized for long periods of time and then so crowded for a short time that the need for expanding them seems apparent to all. Much of this unevenness of demand is unavoidable in view of the rigidity of most people's work schedules, the length of the school day and year, and the Canadian climate. But there is little question that it could be alleviated to some extent by charging higher prices at peak periods to reflect the higher marginal social costs arising from congestion and the consequent deterioration of service quality; indeed, in some instances it may not pay to charge admission *except* at peak periods.[10]

These factors suggest that a re-examination of the pricing strategy employed in many recreational facilities would be worthwhile. The new Metro Toronto Zoo, for example, illustrates some of the problems that arise in the public pricing of recreation facilities. The basic question of whether the zoo is expected to operate at a profit (not including debt charges for the development of the zoo site) or as a community service that cannot be expected to show profit has not really been answered. Although it is clear that in the long run the zoo is expected to break even on operating costs, the initial level of admission charges did not produce as much revenue as expected. Even so, there were complaints from the public about the high admission charges for a zoo that was built with public funds.

While precise answers to such problems depend on a good many specific factors that cannot be developed here, a few general guidelines may be suggested. For example, if full cost recovery is considered desirable, an initial fee equal to the difference between average and marginal costs could be charged to each potential user in the form of an annual membership fee or season pass. In addition, each time the facility is used an additional charge equal to the marginal cost of using the facility would be charged. This two-part system would both meet revenue requirements and also provide most of the benefits of marginal-cost pricing — the "efficiency conditions" outlined in chapter 3. This system seems especially suitable for facilities like swimming pools and golf courses. If the marginal social cost of an additional user is too low to make collecting an admission fee feasible, except perhaps at peak periods, the annual permit system alone could be used and enforced by some system of spot checks. Provincial and national park systems perhaps afford an example.

An alternative approach might be to levy only the actual use charge on residents, if it is believed they have already contributed to the establishment of the facility in the first place through their taxes and hence have a presumptive right of access, while charging a substantially higher fee to nonresidents. Even if this is the prevailing attitude, however, there is still merit in pricing adequately to remind us all that there is no such thing as free public outdoor recreation; someone always has to pay for it — and there are few more eligible candidates than those who make use of it. Most of the external effects expected from recreation facilities would seem to be taken care of by a policy of subsidized, even free, central city services combined with low rates for children everywhere, especially at nonpeak periods.

PRICING REFUSE COLLECTION

As people become richer, they consume more resources and generate more waste, in both solid and liquid forms. One of the most important functions of local governments is therefore the humble but essential task of removing and disposing of the increasing volume of waste resulting from Canadian prosperity. This section considers briefly the role that more effective public pricing can play in accomplishing this task.

Urban garbage collection is a large and growing business. Close to 80 percent of the total costs of solid waste collection and disposal are attributable to collection, and most of the costs of collection are labor costs. The cost of garbage collection, like that of many other urban public services, is thus almost certain to rise in the future as labor continues to become relatively more expensive (see chapter 4) — and people are less easily attracted to such jobs as garbage collecting or even "sanitation engineering."

Garbage collection services supplied to individuals and firms on a private basis are of course generally paid for by fees or charges, like any other service provided through the market. Most refuse collection in Canada, however, is done either directly by municipal authorities or by private firms under municipal contract. In either case, there appear to be few Canadian cities that charge individuals directly for this service. A strong case can, however, be made for charging for this service even when it is provided by a municipal government department.

First, and perhaps most importantly, correctly charging for refuse collection will, by imposing the full social costs of waste generation on those who generate it, aid in obtaining the economically efficient level of waste generation.[11] Charges must therefore reflect not only the costs of collection but also the costs of ultimate treatment and disposal. Unless such a system of charges is established, our society will continue to produce and consume an excessive amount of economic goods in an excessively wasteful and over-packaged way.

A second argument for levying proper charges for refuse collection is that such charges will lead to a more efficient allocation of resources *within* the waste management sector. If the charges are too low, or the service too good for a given level of charges, an excessive amount of waste will have to be collected and subsequently treated or otherwise disposed of. If the charges are too high, or the service too inconvenient, the use of such substitutes as garbage disposal units or littering, which create their own disposal problems, will be unduly encouraged. Only when charges vary correctly with the use of the service will resources be deployed efficiently among these various alternatives.

As noted earlier, a third advantage of pricing is that it provides signals enabling management to provide the appropriate service levels and quality. The other side of this coin is that service charges permit the accommodation of individual preferences — for example, more frequent collections — within any organizational framework, provided, of course, that the collection agency can adequately determine the additional costs and that it has the incentive to provide the requested services on payment of the special charges. This feature is particularly important for commercial and industrial establishments, but it might also be made available to those residents who are willing to pay for it. The point here is that only with an operational pricing mechanism can the individual user influence the service that he gets in any way other than through the cumbersome blunderbuss of the political process. Such a system should be more efficient than the present nonprice rationing system that usually divides users roughly by classes such as type of establishment and district, and supplies the same service to all, whether it is what they want or not.

Corresponding to these three principal advantages of pricing there are three principal problems. The first arises because there are, in fact, significant external aspects of refuse collection or, more pungently, noncollection! Some of these externalities are really neighborhood effects, while others are more general. Such obvious direct effects of refuse collection as the elimination of odors and health hazards are largely spatially confined in nature and therefore fall into the first class of neighborhood effects. In addition, however, "to the extent that a poorly maintained living environment is broadly detrimental to human development and social stability, the provision of universal adequate sanitation is desirable" (Young 1972, p. 59). If health and other hazards are reduced by more frequent removal of refuse, the value of these external benefits should be deducted from the cost to be recouped by user charges.

A more complicated, three-level system of financing may therefore be required to deal with all aspects of the refuse collection problem. In the first place, an area-wide authority, a provincial or regional government, might prescribe minimum standards throughout the area and establish a set of subsidies financed from general revenues that would permit local communities to meet these standards, given the physical and demographic characteristics that affect the costs to them of doing so.[12]

Local areas could impose higher standards if they were willing to pay for them out of their own resources. Finally, individuals could select and pay for still higher service levels than are generally offered in their local area, if they so desire. Any initial subsidies in this system could be provided either out of general tax revenues or out of external cross-subsidization. The latter approach may seem less desirable because it would raise the price of the service to some users above cost, thus distorting waste management practices. But taxes have their own distorting effects, and the best choice is by no means clear. Nevertheless, it is clearly both possible and desirable to couple a pricing system at the level of the individual user with general financing of the externalities of solid waste collection and disposal, if this is what is wanted.

A second problem that is always raised with regard to pricing is that it is seldom clear exactly what the correct charges are or how they can be administered. In fact, however, it would not seem all that difficult to devise and implement charges — for example, by the container — that would be approximately correct in economic terms. A recent American study suggested a basic volume charge covering disposal costs, a charge for collection costs increasing with distance and decreasing with density, and a marginal-cost charge for extra volume (Downing and Gustely 1975). Any such system should probably be implemented on an experimental basis first, say, in one section of a city only, in order to "learn by doing."

A more basic problem with the charging approach is that one cannot really charge for some of the more undesirable substitutes for collection such as littering, accumulating refuse, and unauthorized dumping. All that can be done is to require that all residents subscribe to an adequate refuse removal service ("compelled purchasers") and to devise and implement an effective policing and penalty system to discourage delinquency. To be effective, the expected penalty, the actual penalty times the probability of being caught, has to be high enough to make compliance with the law an attractive alternative.

The third argument against charging is another old perennial — the alleged regressivity of charging for such basic public services as collecting the garbage. The first point to make here is, as usual, to note emphatically that the poverty problem is in no significant sense alleviated by failing to charge for refuse collection. Indeed, it seems quite probable that any minor equity gains from foregoing a charge of, say, $60 per year or so will be offset by the economic inefficiency of nonprice rationing. This point is reinforced if one remembers that *someone* has to pay for the service and that there is little reason to think that local taxes are much, if any, less regressively distributed than service charges would be. Further, it deserves mention that the distributive results of the present nonprice rationing system do not noticeably appear to favor the poor. It is the middle-class districts that complain the most about service quality in this as in other areas of public activity,[13] and it is these districts that are most likely to get the benefit of any service inequalities.

There is, in addition, evidence to the effect that refuse removal is more expensive in less densely populated areas, which are often higher-income areas, and that higher-income families produce significantly more waste than lower-income families.[14] Furthermore, the costs per unit of refuse collection are lower for high-rise apartments than for single-family homes. In these circumstances the imposition of a charging system would make the better off pay more fairly for what service they get, with the net result being a more, rather than less, favorable distributive impact on the poor, whose taxes would no longer go to finance middle-class services. Even if these arguments are ignored and the problem of regressive service charges is felt to add intolerably to the financial burdens of the really poor, it would seem easy enough to adjust welfare payments or tax credits to cover these charges along with other necessary expenditures.

To sum up, the major problem with implementing an adequate set of charges for refuse collection arises neither from equity nor externalities but from such essentially administrative, but none the less important, matters as the correct level of charges, and how best to apply them. The best way to handle such problems is probably to try to do so, preferably on an experimental or small-scale basis. Given the increasing load of garbage swamping our urban areas, it seems high time for some innovative experimentation of this sort to take place in at least some large Canadian cities. Unfortunately, there is little incentive for the present bureaucratic and political structure to even consider, let alone adopt, such radical methods.

PRICING WATER

Many Canadian cities provide their inhabitants, either directly or through municipal enterprises, with such services as electricity, water, sewage disposal, and transportation. These are all essentially private goods and obviously can and should be priced. The economic objective in such pricing is of course to induce people to use resources efficiently; as noted earlier, this is achieved by marginal-cost pricing in order to induce users to impose costs on the system only when it is worth doing so. But the prices set for urban services have social and financial objectives also. The social objective is usually to promote income redistribution and to share costs fairly. The financial objective is to cover costs. Even a brief examination of service pricing in Canada — for example, water pricing — suggests that these objectives have in most cases been ranked in the reverse order, with most attention to covering costs, a little attention to distributional considerations, and almost none to efficiency (Grima 1972). There are, for example, many ways of covering costs — for example, a fixed levy per property served — that do not encourage economy in the use of the system because there are no cost consequences from changing usage.

The effects of the usual urban water pricing policies are almost all undesirable. In the first place, the common use of a declining block rate, a sort of quantity discount, leads to small users subsidizing large users. Some-times lower-income consumers in this way subsidize higher-income con-sumers who have dishwashers, bigger lawns to sprinkle, two cars to wash, and so on. More importantly, as a rule, all residential consumers tend to subsidize industrial users. The only apparent reason for thus favoring in-dustry is the characteristic local government fear that large firms might otherwise choose to leave or not locate in their community; equity and effi-ciency, it appears, are less important than industry.

Given that urban water is an increasingly scarce good, to therefore sub-sidize its consumption makes no sense. In particular, it makes no sense to interpret a shortage of such an underpriced good as requiring substantial new capital investments to increase the supply of water. One of the most important results of pricing water below its marginal cost is to encourage overinvestment in water supply, with consequent unnecessary strain on municipal exchequers. Since the usual bureaucratic incentives to expand operations presumably exist in water utilities in any case, there seems no need to gild the lily in this fashion.

Several studies have shown that, apart from industrial uses, lawn sprinkling is the principal determinant of the peak loads on the water system, and that, as a result, the capacity of water systems has to be much larger than would be otherwise necessary (Hanke 1972). Seasonal pricing would therefore help to regulate water use, and hence check the apparent need for more investment in expanded water systems. Moreover, there is a good deal of evidence that summer sprinkling demand is both income- and price-elastic, which means that subsidizing it, as under the present rate structure, in effect increases the real income of the well-to-do, particularly those with large lawns. It is far from clear why the general taxpayer should thus subsidize private lawns and swimming pools, particularly when the form of subsidy (low marginal water prices) leads to expanded peak de-mand, which in turn requires expensive additional capacity to service it.

Water should, therefore, as one writer has noted, cost more in July than in December, just as Friday night theatre tickets cost more than Wed-nesday night tickets. "These are sound pricing practices which businessmen understand, but which somehow seem beyond the comprehension of some municipal authorities" (Kafoglis 1970, p. 83); or, one might add, apparently beyond many businessmen in this context. Municipal authorities are not necessarily the most culpable in this respect, however. Insofar as water is bought by distributing municipalities from a regional water authority at a flat rate, there is little incentive for them to reduce peak demands, unless the authority itself levies, for example, a summer charge for heavy demands. As is often the case in Canada, better provincial policies are thus an essen-tial prerequisite for better municipal policies.

Finally, the cost of providing many public services is directly related to the density of population in the area being served. While the evidence on this point is far from complete, the costs of providing street service, sewage disposal, water supply, storm sewers, fire protection, and perhaps refuse disposal all appear to vary inversely with the location and characteristics of the area being served, with density being one of the main characteristics.[15] In other words, the outlying, low-density parts of most urban areas are more expensive to serve than the central areas. It therefore follows that correct marginal-cost pricing of these urban services would result in *higher* rates being charged in these areas, rather than the same rates, as is now the usual practice.[16] Furthermore, unless such higher prices are charged, the result of undercharging will be the capitalization of the subsidy in land values so that the level of suburban land values will be higher than would otherwise prevail. If the land were on the margin between agricultural and residential use, the provision of water or other services at prices less than marginal cost would result in higher land values and an increased rate of conversion of fringe land to residential uses. Improper pricing of municipal services is therefore one factor contributing to urban sprawl. The differential bias thus imparted to location decisions may be small for any one service, but the cumulation of many such biases might well be decisive. The possibility of such undesirable and unwarranted biases in urban land-development patterns reinforces the important conclusion that services such as water must not only be priced, but that they must be priced *correctly*, which generally means as close to marginal cost as possible.[17]

EDUCATIONAL FINANCE

Some different aspects of pricing come up with respect to services such as education. Even though educational finance is not under direct municipal control, it impinges heavily on municipal fiscal resources. The present section therefore considers briefly some of the issues and choices currently facing educational finance in Canada.

The history of public financing of elementary and secondary education in most parts of Canada is long and convoluted.[18] Understanding this unique historical evolution is, of course, highly relevant to any consideration of the problems and prospects of the system of educational finance in any particular province. In all provinces, however, circumstances have changed, and it is important today to consider the issues in financing education in the context of the evolving provincial-municipal system as a whole, particularly the financial dimensions of that system. In particular, not only the sorts of "reforms" in educational financing that have often been proposed within the existing system but also much more radical proposals for change need to be considered. Even if some of the latter seem too far removed from reality — at least as "reality" is currently perceived by the majority of those most closely concerned with the educational sector in Canada — to be taken seriously right now, the pressures on the existing way in which education is financed are such that attitudes will probably change within the next decade or so. At the very least, it will become increasingly clear that how a service is financed affects how that service is provided, and, indeed, what service is provided. The increased pressure on the existing educational finance system is likely to result not only in changes in how we *finance* education but also in the *education* that we finance. This interdependence of fiscal and educational policy choices must be taken explicitly into account if wise decisions are to be made in either arena.

These pressures on the present mixed provincial-local system of finance come from two principal sources — the general financial situation and the key role of the property tax in the present system of financing education.

The great postwar expansion in educational spending was made possible largely by the prolonged period of economic expansion up to the early 1970s and by the accompanying virtually painless expansion of provincial government revenues. These were also the years of enormous increases in federal transfers to the provinces, transfers that facilitated and encouraged the marked provincial willingness to finance expanding educational expenditures. The slowing down of economic growth and the new awareness of the tax cost of government suggest that this well has now run dry.

Current indications are that the real revenues at the disposal of most provincial governments are likely to grow considerably more slowly in the future than they did in the past. This slower "automatic" growth of revenues at a time of considerable public sensitivity to discretionary tax increases suggests that provincial expenditures in general will also be constrained over the next decade. The somber prospects for educational finance are reinforced both by the apparently obvious justification for cuts provided by declining school enrolments and by the apparent disillusionment in society with the oversold virtues of the educational panacea; though the latter argument perhaps applies most strongly to the case of post-secondary education.

For various reasons, then — the general economic constraint on provincial revenues, the apparent additional political constraint on provincial expenditures, the decline in the student population, and perhaps also some public dissatisfaction with the educational system — there would appear to be little or no prospect of significantly increased provincial financing of elementary and secondary education in the near future.

This line of argument thus suggests that either the total amount of resources in the educational sector will have to contract or else new sources of finance will have to be found. The only other major source of finance presently utilized is the municipal property tax. The question therefore becomes whether more revenues can or should be derived from this source. And if, as many seem to think (see chapter 5), they cannot or should not be; and yet if the absolute level of education expenditures is to be maintained in real terms, where else can we look? To answer these questions requires a clearer perception of the nature of the provincial-municipal system and of the highly political nature of property tax policy (see also chapter 5).

In principle, of course, school boards may simply levy increased school taxes on municipalities as they see fit. In practice, school boards too are generally elected and hence sensitive to the general feeling against property taxes. Whether this feeling is justified or not does not really matter, since it is, as always, perceptions that govern political actions. But school boards too are under the same need as municipalities to raise taxes in order to maintain service levels. Although the pressure on boards in some respects should be alleviated as a result of declining enrolments, it may actually be increased if, as suggested above, the slowdown in provincial financing hits them more severely.

Moreover, although the effects of the decline in enrolment on costs should cushion the blow somewhat, it is unlikely to offer much relief to hard-pressed school boards in the short run in view of the fixed contractual nature of most costs and the probable upward pressures on wage levels (see chapter 4). Even after such mutual accommodation as can be made locally, the combined pressure of increased school levies *and* increased municipal levies seems almost certain to raise property tax levels significantly in many municipalities. The only way to avoid this result, which past evidence suggests is likely to prove politically unacceptable, would appear to be by making some basic changes in the present system or by cutting sharply the real level of expenditure on education.

The almost certain upshot of any reduction in provincial financing of education is more reliance on property tax finance. There is no economic reason why the property tax structure, whether reformed or not, cannot bear such an increased load (see chapter 5). But what seems more questionable in the current climate is whether the taxpayers, or the provincial governments, which have committed themselves so heavily to the proposition that the property tax is a bad tax, would stand for it.

Aside from important political factors discouraging heavier property taxes, there are, as noted in chapter 5, good reasons for supporting more local financing of local services and for relying heavily on property taxes to supply this financing. It does not follow, however, that an increased share of educational finance should come from the property tax, largely because education is not really a "local" service. Indeed, the heavy provincial involvement in education from the very beginning suggests clear awareness of the "general" rather than purely local nature of the effects of highly unequal local educational systems.

Although it could be argued that increased direct local influence over the content and nature of local educational systems would be desirable, a move in this direction would constitute such a radical break from the tendency of recent years that it is unlikely to take place. The more likely outcome of the pressures sketched above is therefore an increased demand on local property taxpayers to finance a school system over which they have virtually no control. Increased reliance on local financing in this way, however, would result not in increased local autonomy but in reduced political responsibility and accountability, owing both to the severance of the spending school boards from the taxing municipalities and to the vast and detailed provincial influence over board expenditures. All in all, then, increased property taxes for school purposes within the present structure seem both politically unlikely and, at best, questionably desirable.

It would be technically quite possible to shift the basis of local support for education to an income tax base (see also chapter 5). Perhaps the most feasible system would be one in which, as now, provincial grants and controls guaranteed a basic standard of education throughout the province, while the different regions levied differential supplemental income tax rates to make up the difference between this "foundation" standard and that which they chose to achieve. Assuming an appropriate administrative system could be worked out, the consequence would be income tax differentials within the province — probably, like those within the country as a whole now, with the highest rates in the poorest areas but the highest level of educational spending in the richest areas. There is no way to avoid this result without suppressing all possibilities of higher-income regions of providing better levels of education.

Realistically, there seems little reason to think that the province would be willing to permit the establishment of such a regional income tax system. The constant complaints of the provincial governments that the federal government has not provided adequate income tax "room" does not suggest that they would readily give up the room they have to either municipalities or school boards. What may be more likely is the assignment of some portion, fixed or variable, of the income tax yield, or perhaps of the sales tax, to municipal or educational purposes.

If the revenues thus derived are returned to the areas that provide them, the scheme is much like that mentioned above, with the very important difference that there is now no regional discretion on rates; either the resulting variations in funding would have to be offset by grants, or widely different levels of finance for education would result in different regions. If, on the other hand, the revenue produced by this levy were distributed in accordance with any other formula, the system in effect would become just another form of grant rather than any real form of tax sharing (see chapter 7).

In either case, there is really no local role in determining how much should be raised in this way. More importantly in the present context, there is also no reason to expect that any resources secured for education through such devices would be additions rather than simply replacements for other grants or property taxes.

In any case, increased provincial grants to education in any form seem rather unlikely in present circumstances. The complete provincial takeover of education might therefore seem to be an even more unlikely solution to the educational finance problem. Nevertheless, the idea is worth discussing here because it is an eminently logical extension of the apparent trend of educational policy in Canada since the Second World War. The only significant argument against it — apart from its financial implications — is that it would reduce the scope for local input and local diversity in the educational system. At the present time, however, the real scope for either is already minuscule. Moreover, it is possible, at least in principle, to retain and even enhance such local input in a completely provincial educational system, as set out, for example, in Nova Scotia (1974). The battle for local control of education was lost long ago in most of the country, indeed virtually before it could be fought. Why not go all the way and recognize that education is now basically a provincial rather than a local service?

Full provincialization of education would thus represent simply a further step along a path Canada has been following for many years. The main financial argument against it — that the absence of the visible property tax constraint on local boards would remove any incentive to restrain educational expenditures — makes sense only to those who believe that provincial governments do not have similar incentives, particularly these days. A move in this direction would also have the substantial advantage of separating the question of the appropriate level of educational spending from the question of the appropriate level of the property tax.

This is not to say, however, that property taxes would necessarily be reduced as a result of such a shift. On the contrary, the contribution of property taxes to educational finance is probably much too large for the provincial government to forego this revenue source completely if it were to take on the full burden of financing education. One possible scenario — that proposed in Nova Scotia (1974) — would be for the province to take over all the nonresidential property tax, which coincidentally produces about the right amount of revenue, leaving the residential portion of the tax to finance general municipal services. Such a move would make much more valid the common perception of the residential property tax as a benefit tax (see chapter 5). It would also be consistent with the persistently displayed provincial interest in removing much of the burden of the more expensive "general" services from the residential property tax.[19]

The scenario sketched above would result in the following realignment of functions and finances: The municipalities would levy taxes on residential property for general services — and, ideally, make much more use of service and user charges on residents and businesses alike. The provinces would completely finance and control elementary and secondary education, obtaining the additional financial resources through the taxation of nonresidential property, or in any other way they saw fit. The school boards would remain as basically local advisory committees; they would have no direct taxing role at all but might retain substantial, perhaps even increased, expenditure responsibility if some adequate form of output monitoring could be devised (Nova Scotia 1974).

A number of important obscurities clearly remain in this picture. Just how would the school boards function? Could they be effective if they had no direct taxing role? Would the removal of nonresidential property from the local tax base adversely affect municipal land-use decisions? . . . and so on. Nevertheless, this system has several major virtues that suggest it would repay more careful examination. It would make the lines of responsibility clear, and closer to reality than in the present system; it would separate the property tax and educational issues; and, finally, despite its radical appearance, it is in fact really a logical outgrowth of the long-standing trend towards the provincial provision and finance of education and provincial control of the property tax.

An even more radical way of coping with present educational finance realities may be called the "Economist's Solution" (Buttrick 1977) of devising a financial mechanism that in effect permits individual parents to have some *direct* say on the level and nature of the education obtained by their children.

When the quantity of educational services demanded declines owing to a fall in enrolment, elementary economics suggests that the quantity of such services supplied should also decline. Much of the "problem" seen by educators arises from their desire to continue devoting the same, or even more per pupil, resources to education in the face of this fall in market demand. The present bureaucratic provision of public education in effect makes it almost unresponsive to such demand shifts. The real consumers of the educational product in a market sense are not the public, who "buy" it only at several removes, but governments, and in particular the provincial government. The public affect the decision of government as to how much education to buy only through their actions at the polls and that nebulous but important force called "public opinion."

The problem facing educators today is that, for the first time in decades, they are coming to realize that not everyone wants to buy more of what they have to sell. The psychic shock of learning this unpleasant fact, coupled with the real human difficulties faced by all producers in declining industries, may make it seem almost cruel to discuss the possibility of introducing direct market forces even more openly into the educational picture. In fact, however, it may be argued that *only* by doing so is there much prospect of *increasing* the resources going to the educational sector in the near future, should this be determined to be an appropriate policy goal. This prospect is perhaps attractive enough to warrant closer examination even by those most wedded to the present virtually monopolistic bureaucratic educational system. Those who want more variety and choice than is now afforded to parents and students by that system should of course find the market-oriented options even more interesting.[20]

Broadly speaking, there are three ways in which a more explicit "market" in school services might be introduced on the demand side: through fees, tax credits, or educational vouchers. The first of these methods of charging full cost to parents has the usual economic merits of pricing, but in the absence of an adequate basic income redistributional policy it is probably a nonstarter (Seldon 1977).

The second method allows parents or students to credit fees, or some portion of them, against taxes, thus providing a uniform subsidy to education. In principle this system can achieve exactly the same results as a system of direct grants to all schools — not just publicly provided schools — for the equivalent fraction of educational costs (Stubblebine 1965). Again, however, unless the tax credits are made fully refundable, in the form of negative income tax, the basic distributional problem makes it difficult to consider this alternative seriously.

The best "market-oriented" system available, then, appears to be what are called "educational vouchers," which are, in effect, nontransferable subsidies that may be spent only on education. The main difference from the present system is that these vouchers would not have to be spent in state-provided schools. The differences from the other "market" systems mentioned above are that the vouchers would have to be spent on education, and that the amount of the voucher could be made *inverse* to income, if desired. The compulsory and subsidization aspects of the present system could thus be retained, and indeed the degree of redistribution through education could even be enhanced.

Indeed, only the poor might receive vouchers, with the rich being left to look after themselves. If such overt pro-poor discrimination were thought to be politically unpalatable, equal vouchers could be given to all; the result would of course be unequal educational opportunities for the children of the rich and poor, though there is no reason to think that the resulting inequality would be any greater than that prevailing under the present system where, in effect, the same situation prevails. The only difference with a voucher system would be that parents could, within the limits of their other resources, transportation possibilities, and the like, *choose* where to spend their educational money.

The main implications of this approach to financing education are thus for the supply of education. This is not the place to pursue the many arguments on this aspect in detail. Various scenarios have been sketched in the literature, with perhaps the most probable being a mixed public-private system.[21] In any case, the upshot would almost certainly be a system much more responsive to the wishes of parents, who would now be the *direct* financers of the education system. This increased responsiveness is one of the principal virtues of the voucher approach.

The other virtue, from some points of view, is the probability that the result of enabling parents to exercise more choice with respect to the education of their children may well be an *increase* in the total expenditure on education (Seldon 1977). Even keeping the same basic provision system as now exists in Ontario, it has been suggested that this outcome would be the result of increased student retention in secondary schools (Buttrick 1977).

The principal arguments against vouchers are that the outcome would almost certainly be more overt if not real inequality in educational opportunity (Klappholz 1972). Overstated as this argument usually is — if 100 years of compulsory education has not educated the populace to the point of rationally choosing education for their children, more such education would appear to be of little social utility — there is some merit in this reproach. On the other hand, the opportunity to create centers of different kinds of excellence will no longer be confined to the very well-off alone, which in turn might be taken to improve opportunity. Nevertheless, different choices will indeed result in different, and unequal educational opportunities, and the rich will no doubt come out best in this, as in any other scheme. This result clearly goes against the long-standing desire in Canada to equalize educational opportunities across and within jurisdictions.

Another argument against vouchers appears to be even more crucial in the eyes of some. It is that education is not, and should not be, left to the choice of parents because it provides the important social underpinnings of value inculcation, and hence must be under the control of the state — or at least the control of the certified state educator. In fact, through curriculum and training control the same ends can be achieved, to the extent that they are considered socially desirable, through a private system as well, as indeed Ontario experience with separate schools shows. What *cannot* be so achieved, however, is the thorough homogenization of the population that is the apparent aim of some educators (Rowley 1969).

As these remarks suggest, the choice of any of the "market" alternatives to the present system of educational finance would raise even more fundamental problems in educational and social philosophy than would a complete provincial takeover. Partly for this reason, the latter seems a more likely and desirable outcome in the near future than any sort of educational "pricing" system. Nevertheless, either approach — provincialization or pricing — would have the substantial advantage over the present system of bringing together educational responsibility and authority at one decision level instead of the present uneasy compromise between provincial governments, municipal authorities, and school boards — with citizens, as a rule, having little direct involvement at any level.

7 Provincial-Municipal Transfers

How local governments fit into the overall provincial-municipal system has been discussed in previous chapters. Municipalities in Canada are very much creatures of the province. Although the precise nature of provincial intervention varies substantially from province to province, it is nevertheless true everywhere that the services local governments are allowed or required to provide, the standards they have to maintain, and how they finance them, are all largely determined at the provincial level of government.

This chapter considers another way in which the province exerts considerable control over local decisions — through provincial-municipal transfers. By specifying how these funds must be spent, the province attaches strings to one of the most important sources of revenues of local governments. In the next section, a brief description of the various types of transfers is followed by a discussion of the rationales for transfers. Then follows a discussion of the impact of transfers on local decision making.

TYPES OF TRANSFERS

The two major categories of transfers, or grants, are unconditional — those that have no restrictions attached to their use — and conditional — those that require certain conditions to be met by the recipient. Conditional grants can be further broken down into matching and nonmatching grants. A matching grant is one in which the donor pays a certain specified percentage of expenditures made on a particular function. For example, the province may offer to pay 70 percent of expenditures on a particular transportation facility, leaving the remaining 30 percent to be financed by the municipality. The municipality is, in a sense, paying for the facility with 30-cent dollars. Nonmatching grants are "lump-sum" transfers and require no funds to be put up by the recipient. An example of a nonmatching grant is a per capita grant.

Another distinction that may be drawn is between open-ended and closed-ended grants. Open-ended grants do not specify an upper dollar limit on the amount of grant funds available. Closed-ended grants, on the other hand, place a limit on the funds the municipality can receive. In addition to specified dollar limits, that is, explicitly closed-ended, grants can be implicitly closed-ended by other means, for example, by requiring provincial approval of the expenditures or by defining eligible costs to be less than total costs.

Finally, grants may be designated specifically for capital purposes or for operating purposes. For example, some grants may only be used for maintenance, while others may only be used to build a particular facility.

As shown in chapter 5, the majority of provincial-municipal grants in Canada are conditional (specific purpose) rather than unconditional (general purpose). Most grants have to be spent on projects specified by the provincial donors and in ways designated by the relevant provincial authorities. In this way, the provinces are able to maintain considerable control over what appear to be local expenditure functions. This control is executed by defining eligible costs, by imposing copious rules and regulations, and by altering the price of certain services to the municipality. The result is that municipalities provide many local public services themselves, but the standards are, in effect, set by the provinces.

An idea of the complexity of grant programs can be obtained from Appendix A, which illustrates the various types of grants existing in Ontario in 1979; the table includes only a little more than one-third of the grant programs.[1] Although the system in Ontario is more elaborate than in other provinces, the general picture of complexity suggested by this Appendix is probably not seriously misleading.[2]

Some grants are received by municipalities directly, others go to municipal boards or agencies. Grants are administered by different provincial departments or ministries; not surprisingly, each department has different rules and regulations that must be followed. Even within a particular grant program, the grant formula often varies depending on the particular circumstances of the recipient municipality. As a rule, each grant program has some unique feature, whether it be the formula, the conditions, or other rules or procedures, to distinguish it from other grants.

Two general conclusions can be drawn concerning provincial-municipal grants in Canada. The first is that most such grants are conditional, and the second is that the provinces maintain considerable control over local finances through these conditional grant programs. As noted in chapter 5, most provincial grants to municipalities are conditional, or specific-purpose transfers, and most of these are for education. Also, most of these grants are closed-ended, with explicit or implicit limits set by the provincial governments. This, in conjunction with the overall complexity of the grant system, suggests the significant provincial control over taxing and spending decisions. That conclusion is further strengthened when one also considers the empirical evidence on the impact of provincial-local grants on expenditure decisions of local governments as discussed later in this chapter.

RATIONALES FOR TRANSFERS

The theory of fiscal federalism outlined briefly in chapter 3 provides two principal economic rationales for intergovernmental transfers — allocative efficiency, to affect the level or mix of expenditures, and fiscal equity, to equalize revenues between recipient governments. In addition, a number of other justifications, mostly noneconomic, for why grants exist have been outlined in the literature.

The provision of a public service in one jurisdiction may result in spillover benefits or costs to residents of other jurisdictions. Examples of activities that generate interjurisdictional spillovers include education and transportation. A person may be educated in one jurisdiction and then move to another jurisdiction, taking the benefits of his education with him. Similarly, a highway constructed through one jurisdiction may benefit those in neighboring jurisdictions as well. An example of an external cost would be water pollution. If one jurisdiction does not clean up its part of the river, costs of pollution are created for jurisdictions downstream.

Such interjurisdictional spillovers (externalities) can potentially lead to a misallocation of resources. As discussed in chapter 3, the jurisdiction providing the public service generally only considers the benefits and costs for its own residents when it determines how much to supply. For example, in the highway case, the benefits to residents commuting from neighboring jurisdictions would not necessarily be considered. Although the particular jurisdiction has no incentive to consider the external benefits or costs of the public service on other jurisdictions, society as a whole will be better off if all of the benefits and costs, regardless of where they occur, are considered by the jurisdiction.

Where external benefits exist, some sort of mechanism is required to encourage expansion of the activity to account for these external effects. A subsidy to the jurisdiction generating the spillover could achieve this goal.[3] The type of subsidy required is an open-ended matching grant, one in which the donor pays a certain specified percentage of the expenditures on the particular service, and there is no limit to the amount of the grant. The matching rate, percentage of expenditures, in principle should represent the ratio of external benefits to total benefits. For example, if one-fifth of the total benefits of a service spill over into other jurisdictions, then the matching rate would be 20 percent; the donor government pays 20 percent of the expenditures on that activity, and the recipient government pays the remaining 80 percent. By altering the price of the public service to the jurisdiction providing it, the grant provides some incentive to expand the public service. The grant is open-ended on the assumption that spillover benefits increase as long as expenditures increase.

The second rationale for intergovernmental grants stated above is on fiscal equity grounds. This objective requires that each jurisdiction be able to provide some "average" level of public services by exerting an "average" fiscal effort, usually measured as its tax rate.

One jurisdiction may not be able to provide the same level of public services at the same tax rate as another jurisdiction. There may be many reasons for this. For example, tax bases differ from jurisdiction to jurisdiction. To collect the same amount of revenue, a jurisdiction with a low tax base will have to levy a higher tax rate than one with a large tax base. Another reason may be that the costs of providing certain public services are higher in one jurisdiction than in another, so that a larger tax yield may be required to provide the same level of public services. Finally, the need for particular public services may be greater in one jurisdiction than another, thereby necessitating larger expenditures and consequently a greater tax yield in that jurisdiction.

One way to achieve this goal of fiscal equity is by providing sufficient lump-sum grants to the poorer regions so that all regions can provide a given level of public services at the same rate of tax. These grants should be unconditional, in that the recipient is not required to spend the funds on any particular public service. They should also be lump-sum, which means that the recipient does not have to match the funds of the donor government. Such grants, in practice, usually vary according to such criteria as the need and taxable capacity (ability of jurisdictions to raise taxes, usually measured by its tax base) of the jurisdiction. The precise formulas depend on the specific equalization objectives of the donor government.[4]

In addition to the above justifications for transfers, the literature suggests a number of other reasons why grants exist. Unconditional transfers, for example, are often justified simply on the ground that senior levels of government have greater revenue-raising capabilities than their lower-level counterparts. Local governments, for example, have only a restricted taxing ability because both labor and capital can avoid their taxes by moving to another jurisdiction. It is somewhat more difficult to avoid a tax imposed by the central government. The central government thus has greater ability to levy taxes. There are also economies of scale in tax administration that can be more adequately taken advantage of by a central government. Lower levels of government often face a mismatch of revenues and expenditures because expenditure demands are rising far more quickly than are revenues, at given tax rates. There is thus a "fiscal gap" between spending responsibilities and taxing powers (Boadway 1980). One way to close this gap is by giving unconditional lump-sum transfers to increase the revenues of lower-level governments.

There may, however, be better ways to solve the problem of a mismatching of revenues and expenditures. Lower-level governments could, for example, be provided with such additional revenue sources as an income tax or sales tax. There could be more adequate revenue sharing with the upper-level governments or, alternatively, certain expenditure functions could be transferred to another level of government that has greater revenues to finance them. Grants are only one way to meet expenditure requirements when local revenues are inadequate.

Another argument for intergovernmental transfers is that upper-level governments may want local governments to provide their own services for administrative or other reasons, but at the same time they want to maintain control over how the money is spent and to establish certain minimum levels of these services (Gramlich 1976). One instrument for achieving this dual purpose is a conditional matching grant that is closed-ended. Through this device, the donor government may alter the price of particular public services to the recipient municipality, thereby encouraging spending on functions designated by the upper government. By making such grants closed-ended, the donor government is also able to control the amount of funds it gives out in grants. Schultze (1974) argues that such transfers can be thought of as a device whereby local governments act as agents or contractors for the donor governments in carrying out specific tasks.

Breton and Scott (1978) have proposed a "positive" theory of grants based on the concept that bureaucrats and politicians are essentially self-interested (see chapter 3). They argue that the central government has surplus tax revenues because it has greater taxing powers relative to expenditure requirements than do local levels of government.[5] The lower levels of government have inadequate revenues to meet their expenditure needs. The result is that those levels of government with surplus tax revenues are assumed to enter an imagined trade as buyers of "expenditure functions," while those with inadequate tax revenues enter as sellers of these functions. Grants are, in this way, treated as "the price of traded functions."

The payments for these functions can take several different forms, including conditional or unconditional transfers, the type depending on the interaction of the politicians and the bureaucrats. Politicians who are giving out the grants are probably indifferent, but their bureaucrats will likely tend to prefer conditional grants because they require greater co-ordination and administration costs. In other words, conditional grants require the services of more bureaucrats. Politicians who receive grants prefer unconditional ones because they allow greater flexibility but, again, their bureaucrats may prefer the administratively more complex conditional grants. Breton and Scott conclude that donors will often give in to the wishes of bureaucrats and opt for conditional grants, but recipients, preferring greater flexibility, will not be so indulgent of their bureaucrats and will therefore prefer unconditional grants. The final outcome will depend upon the relative bargaining strengths of the donors and recipients.

This argument is more an explanation of why grants exist than a rationale for why grants *should* exist. As noted previously, there are always other ways to compensate for surplus revenues at one level of government and inadequate revenues at another.

Finally, Winer (1979) rejects the traditional arguments for grants — externalities and redistribution — in favor of a justification that is more political. In his view, the central government gives grants to lower-level governments so that it can be identified with the services provided by the lower-level governments. He describes the procedure whereby grants are given as follows: The central government offers to pay part of the expenditures of each lower-level government in turn — financed by taxing the other lower-level governments. If only one lower-level government accepts the offer, then it will appear to the residents of that jurisdiction that their tax shares have been reduced relative to those in other jurisdictions. Given this version of what is called the "prisoner's dilemma," each lower-level government is in effect forced to accept the offer of the central government to avoid paying for benefits going to others. Overall, the result is that the perceived tax shares remain the same, and the expenditure decisions of the lower-level governments are unaltered.

Other authors looking at intergovernmental transfers in Canada have also argued that such grants tend to be given essentially for political reasons rather than for purely economic reasons.[6] The most likely rationale for most provincial-municipal transfers appears to be to allow provincial governments to maintain a certain amount of control over the expenditure and taxing decisions of the local governments, while letting the local governments administer many public services. Grants to achieve this end would, as noted above, tend to be closed-ended and matching, and, as seen in Appendix A, most provincial-municipal transfers appear to match this prescription.

IMPACT OF TRANSFERS ON LOCAL DECISION-MAKING

Whatever their rationale may be, it is obviously important to know how these transfers affect the budget decisions of local governments. A vast theoretical and empirical literature has therefore developed to study the fiscal response of local governments to transfers from other levels of government. The main aim of these studies is to determine how the expenditure and tax decisions of the recipient government are affected by intergovernmental transfers. If, for example, a local government receives a grant of $1.00 and it spends more than $1.00 as a result, this is called "stimulation" because the grant has stimulated expenditures and has resulted in an increase in taxes. On the other hand, if a local government receives a grant of $1.00 and it spends less than $1.00, this is called "substitution." The grant has presumably resulted in a reduction in taxes; the grant has been substituted, in effect, for taxes.

The different types of grants are expected, theoretically, to result in different expenditure responses.[7] The usual theory is based on a model of government behavior that assumes the recipient government maximizes the utility of its citizens subject to a budget constraint (usually that total expenditures must equal total revenues).[8] The different types of grants are assumed to alter the revenues of the recipient government and consequently alter its budget constraint in different ways.

Utility is assumed to depend on the aided local public good or service (Q_a) and all other goods and services both private and public (Q_b). Figure 7-1 shows the pregrant equilibrium solution.[9] *AB* represents the budget constraint faced by the municipality before grants are introduced. Equilibrium occurs at point *X*, where utility is maximized (at $U = U°$) subject to the budget constraint *AB*. At this point Ob_1 is purchased of the local good and Oa_1 of all other goods. If we assume constant average costs in the production of the local aided good, and also assume that the local aided good has unit cost, then Ob_1 also represents expenditures on the local aided good.

The introduction of grants into this model alters the budget constraint. Different grants result in different movements of the budget line and conse-

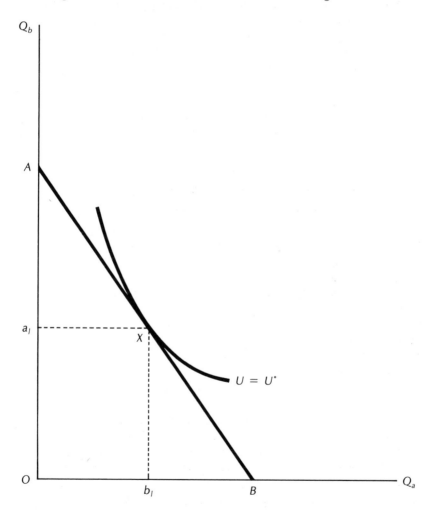

Figure 7-1 Pregrant Equilibrium

quently in different responses by municipalities in terms of the mix of the aided good and other goods that they choose. Consider first an unconditional grant, also called a general nonmatching grant, a lump-sum unconditional grant, or a block grant. This grant can be used for any purpose, to be spent on the local aided good or all other goods, and does not require matching funds to be made by the municipality. The unconditional grant only affects the *income* of the community and not relative prices. Diagrammatically, the budget line shifts from its initial position, represented by *AB* in Figure 7-2, to *CD* (a parallel shift) by the amount of the grant, which is *BD*. Note that the parallel shift in the budget line does not alter the relative prices for the aided good and all other goods faced by the municipality.

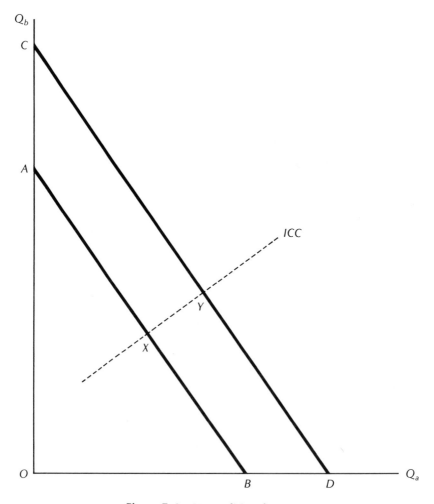

Figure 7-2   Unconditional Grant

Given that neither good is inferior, it is expected that the municipality will now purchase more of both goods. In other words, if both goods have positive income elasticities of demand, the postgrant equilibrium would move out along the income-consumption curve (ICC) to point *Y*. This means that the unconditional grant has resulted in increased expenditures on the aided good, but by an amount less than the grant because expenditures on all other goods have increased.

The second type of grant to consider is the specific nonmatching grant. This grant must be spent on the aided good, but the donor requires no matching funds on the part of the recipient. Since it is nonmatching, there is only an income effect. This is shown in Figure 7-3. The restriction in the use

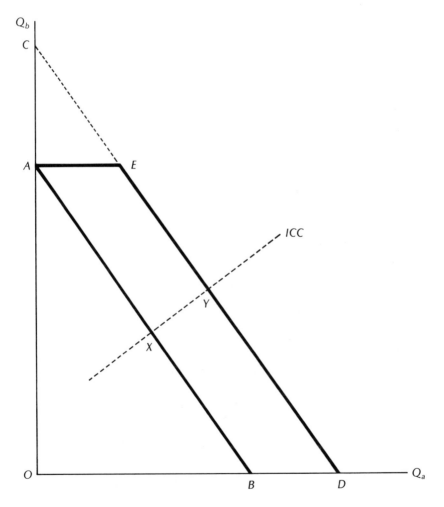

Figure 7-3　Specific Nonmatching Grant

of this grant results in a new kinked budget line *AED*. The amount of all other goods that could be purchased, that is, if none of the aided good was purchased, remains the same as before the grant was introduced, *OA*. Again, if neither good is inferior, the municipality will purchase more of both goods and move to a point like *Y*. The restriction has no effect unless the original position was beyond the kink, in which case the new solution would be at *E*.

Consider next a specific open-ended matching grant where it is restricted to the aided good and the donor pays a specified percentage of the total expenditures. This type of grant alters the price of the aided good to

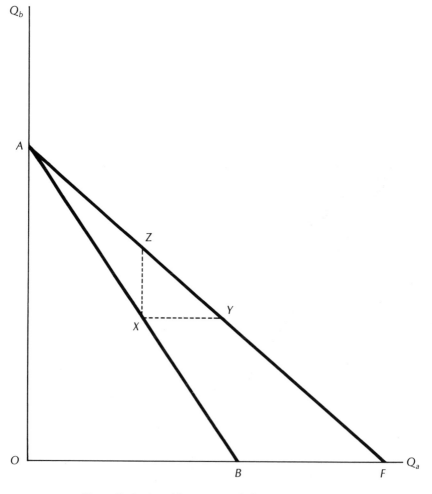

Figure 7-4   Specific Open-ended Matching Grant

the municipality and results in the new budget constraint *AF*, shown in Figure 7–4.

The postgrant equilibrium will be on the new budget constraint *AF*, but the magnitude of the increase in expenditures depends on the price elasticity of demand for the aided good. If the expenditure demand is of unitary elasticity, the price consumption curve is horizontal, and the new equilibrium will be at *Y*, indicating that expenditures increase exactly by the amount of the grant *XY*. Where the expenditure demand is price elastic, the price consumption curve is downward sloping, and total expenditures will increase by more than the amount of the grant, causing expenditures on all

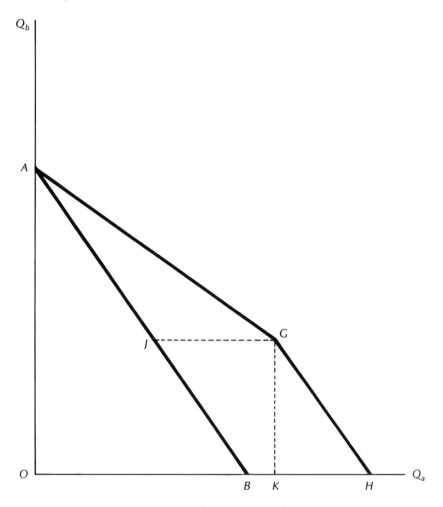

Figure 7-5   Specific Closed-ended Matching Grant

other goods to decline. The new postgrant equilibrium will be somewhere along *YF*. Finally, where the price elasticity of demand is less than one, the price consumption curve is upward sloping and the postgrant equilibrium will be somewhere along *YA*. Total expenditures increase by less than the grant.

A specific closed-ended matching grant is similar to an open-ended one with the exception that a limit is placed on the amount of aid the municipality can receive. In other words, the donor government will finance a certain proportion of expenditures on the aided good up to a specified dollar limit. The new budget line in this case is shown as *AGH* in Figure 7-5. This assumes that the maximum grant a donor will pay is *BH*. If the municipality

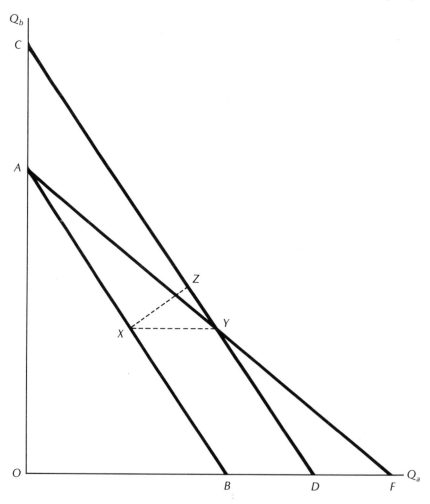

**Figure 7-6   Comparison of Unconditional and Specific
Open-ended Matching Grants**

chooses to purchase more than *OK* of the aided good, the grant remains *BH*. Up until the point where the maximum grant is reached, the specific matching grant will alter relative prices. Beyond the maximum, there is no price effect but rather only an income effect.

Finally, Figure 7–6 compares the impact of an unconditional grant and a specific open-ended matching grant. Figure 7–6 has been drawn so that a grant of constant size *XY* can be used as the basis for comparison. For an unconditional grant *XY*, the new equilibrium will move along the income-consumption curve from point *X* to point *Z*; there is only an income effect. A specific matching grant of the same magnitude *XY* would result in a new budget constraint *AF* and a postgrant equilibrium at *Y*. Point *Y* can be broken down into an income effect and a substitution effect, where the income effect is *XZ* and the substitution effect is *ZY*. By way of comparison, the unconditional grant results in a smaller expenditure response than does the specific matching grant, which has both an income and a substitution effect. Since the substitution effect for the aided good in response to grants is always negative, this negative price effect will always make the response to a specific matching grant greater than the response to an unconditional grant.

EMPIRICAL STUDIES OF LOCAL FISCAL RESPONSE

Econometric studies of intergovernmental transfers explain statistically how grants affect expenditures by using regression analysis to test the impact of grants on expenditures and taxes.

The impact of a grant on the expenditure and tax decisions of a recipient government therefore depends in large part on whether the particular grant has only an income effect or a price and income effect. The theory predicts that the expenditure response will be greatest for conditional, open-ended, matching grants followed by conditional, closed-ended, matching grants.

A vast empirical literature has developed around this question. Early "determinants" studies simply ran linear regressions of several variables, including transfers, on expenditures. More recent studies have devised models of local government behavior, usually based on consumer utility-maximization models, to test the impact of grants on expenditures. Such studies are outlined a little more fully in Appendix B.

Although considerable progress has been made toward resolving many of the conceptual and empirical problems in modeling the impact of grants on local budget decisions, there are still some important limitations in the models being used. One such limitation arises because all of these models assume that politicians maximize the utility of citizens, a somewhat unrealistic assumption. McGuire (1975) postulated instead that bureaucrats respond to price and budget changes in a consistent manner. He contended that budget- or bureau-maximizing behavior (see Niskanen 1971) could also be tested with his model, in which expenditures on the aided function depend on expenditures on the unaided function, the portion of grants not remitting in tax reductions, the ratio of grants to expenditures plus grants, and such usual socioeconomic variables as population. Some further work along these lines was attempted by Feldstein and Frisch (1977), who tested both a political model and a bureaucratic model. Their empirical results suggested that the political model — focusing on factors assumed to influence voting — was more appropriate in describing the budgetary process of schools, at least in the state of Massachusetts.

Another limitation inherent in the usual utility-maximization models is that they assume that the choice of technique for producing the aided good or service is unaffected by grants.[10] This is not necessarily the case, however, with conditional grants. A grant conditional on being used for capital purposes, for example, would make capital relatively cheaper and,[11] consequently, the recipient government may alter its production process for the subsidized good to make it more capital intensive.[12] This behavior could have important implications for the expenditure response to conditional grants. The utility-maximization models implicitly assume that grants do not alter the choice of production technique because they do not distort factor prices. The results of these models, then, only hold for the case where grants do not explicitly subsidize capital, labor, or other specific factors. In reality, many transfer programs — as may be noted in Appendix A — do contain such explicit subsidies to either capital or operating costs.

To summarize, a great number of empirical studies have been done in Canada and elsewhere on the fiscal response of lower-level governments to transfers from upper-level governments. There is still no consensus in the literature, however, concerning the magnitude of the expenditure response to intergovernmental transfers, although it does appear that the theoretical expectations mentioned earlier hold, that is, conditional grants are more likely to induce expenditures on particular services than unconditional grants.

On average, roughly one-half of total local government revenues are derived from transfers (chapter 5). In other words, transfers are as important a revenue source to municipalities as are revenues from own sources that are under local control.[13] As shown earlier in this chapter the majority of provincial-municipal grants in Canada are conditional, closed-ended, matching grants that do not seem appropriate to achieve either allocative efficiency or fiscal equity. Provincial-municipal transfers in Canada thus appear to be designed to allow provincial governments to maintain a fair amount of control over the expenditure and taxing decisions of local governments while appearing to let local governments provide their own services. In effect, local governments in Canada, to a considerable extent, are really acting as agents, spending provincial funds on provincially designated activities.

8 Urban Finance: A New Approach

Cities in Canada as elsewhere have been pressed to spend more and more in recent years to satisfy the needs and demands of their increasing populations. At the same time, however, two trends in contemporary Canada have weakened the ability of Canadian cities to respond to this pressure. Both of these trends arise from the fact that the public sector as a whole has expanded significantly in this period, to the point where over 40 percent of the national income is now channeled through the government in one form or another.

One inevitable accompaniment of this public-sector growth has been an increased centralization of public revenues, at least as seen from the local side. The two principal revenue sources, general sales and income taxes, including payroll taxes — the only taxes that increase more or less automatically along with income — are simply not within the reach of local governments.

A second result of the increased size of the public sector, especially at the provincial level, is that the provincial authorities have, directly and indirectly, come to play a dominant role. To an increasing extent local governments have thus become more subject to provincial influences, both directly through intergovernmental fiscal transfers, controls over local borrowing and local investment decisions, and so on, and indirectly, through the effects of provincial and federal policies on the local economy and on local expenditures and revenues. Cities have therefore been expected to do more and more different things, while at the same time becoming more dependent on provincial largesse and more subject to provincial control.

The result of these multiple forces has been the emergence of a problem that has been variously labeled "fiscal mismatch," "fiscal imbalance," or "fiscal squeeze." By whatever name it is known, the situation described is one in which urban governments find themselves year after year facing rising expenditures and more slowly rising revenues, particularly revenues from sources under their own control (see chapter 2). Even if local resources happen to match local expenditures at some particular moment, the changing times that characterize the modern era almost invariably again throw urban revenues and expenditures out of balance. In the last few years, for example, given the usual lack of response of local revenues to changing price levels, inflation has everywhere exacerbated the urban fiscal dilemma (see chapter 4).

Faced with this situation of fiscal imbalance, the almost invariable response of municipal leaders has been to seek more, and more diverse, sources of fiscal revenue, particularly revenue under local control. A common demand from hard-pressed urban authorities, for example, has been for direct local access to the income tax. This demand is greatly strengthened by the understandable dislike of urban politicians for raising additional revenues through the highly visible, and highly unpopular, property tax (see chapter 5).

A different reaction to urban fiscal pressure has been to shift the responsibility for some of the more costly services, particularly health, education, and welfare, up to higher levels of government. Still another has been to reorganize municipal governments, sometimes allegedly with the idea of realizing economies of scale in the provision of urban public services by consolidating the numerous small political jurisdictions sometimes found in particular metropolitan areas into one large jurisdiction (see chapter 3). Such consolidation has seldom been accompanied by any direct strengthening of the fiscal basis of the new local authority, except to the extent that the inclusion of richer peripheral areas raises the local tax base.

Yet another reaction of central government to the fiscal plight of municipal governments has been, in effect, to increase fragmentation by entrusting the provision of certain urban services to special service districts or special autonomous agencies. Such functional fragmentation invariably weakens both the unity and the fiscal base of the general local authority (see chapter 4). Neither fragmentation of municipal service provision nor municipal reorganization alone really grapples with the essence of the urban fiscal dilemma.

As most city authorities see matters, the basic problem is simply that they do not have sufficient revenues to enable them to carry out the tasks with which they are charged. The required solution is therefore obvious, at least to them—give them the resources they need to do the job. They would prefer, of course, to have these resources under their direct control, but since "beggars can't be choosers," they are, for the most part, prepared to take the money wherever they can get it.

Provincial governments, on the other hand, have generally shown an equally understandable reluctance to give up any direct control over their lucrative tax bases — although they have, albeit usually rather grudgingly, proved willing either to transfer vastly increased funds to local governments, usually on a conditional basis, or to take some expenditure functions off their hands (see chapter 7). In the course of doing so, however, many local authorities feel that provincial governments have used their powers over the purse strings to alter local priorities significantly, with the result that some relevant local needs and diversities have been neglected.

In their innermost hearts, then, most local authorities probably feel that the basic issue of urban finance today is simply to ensure that they, the relevant local authorities, secure the funds needed to carry out those expenditures that they see as required in today's expanding cities. But is this way of looking at things either realistic or useful?

In reality, the problems and pressures may appear to be on urban revenues, but the real problems lie much deeper in the combination of rising population and rising expectations that has characterized postwar Canada. These problems cannot really be usefully discussed from the necessarily limited perspective of the revenue "needs" of urban managers. The urban fiscal dilemma is just one aspect of a basic national dilemma. What is really at issue is the capability of the nation's governmental system as a whole to cope with the changing needs and desires of its populace. Urban finances constitute an integral part of a national system and must therefore be analyzed in this context.

This broader perspective suggests at once that the key to understanding the urban fiscal problem lies not on the revenue but on the *expenditure* side of government budgets. A principal question that should always be asked in this regard — but seldom is — is whether the existing structure of the public sector in fact produces the "right" bundle of goods and services. Does the inevitably imperfect political process result in an appropriate perception of the demand or need for public provision of particular goods and services? And are these perceived demands appropriately satisfied by the goods and services actually provided through the multilayered government bureaucracy? These are among the basic questions of all public finance, not just urban finance (see chapters 3 and 4).

Another important question concerns the extent to which the relationships between different levels of government are presumed to be fixed, and appropriate. Unlike the questions raised immediately above, which are in a sense so "basic" that one can hardly conceive of their being asked by a practising politician or bureaucrat, let alone answered, the appropriateness of the existing order of governments has indeed been examined in detail in Canada recently. The result of this examination at the provincial-municipal level in Canada has almost always been to increase the pace at which centralization was occurring anyway as a consequence of central access to elastic revenue sources and growing central influence over the economy. Yet this conclusion is not at all obviously correct, once the question of whether the governmental structure as a whole is delivering what people really need is taken into account.

The point of raising these very fundamental issues here is simply to emphasize the need to remember, that urban fiscal problems constitute just one aspect of the basic public finance question of designing the national fiscal system that will best achieve the objectives of society as a whole. The fact that particularly strong pressures show up on the revenue side of the urban fiscal budget does not necessarily mean that the solution to these problems necessarily lies in their direct alleviation by giving cities more revenues. What may be happening is that the governmental system as a whole may be misallocating resources, with consequent effects on, say, industrial location and employment patterns, and hence local finances, or in such a way as to give rise to increased citizen discontent, which materializes in the local context. In these circumstances, what may be needed are adjustments to *national* revenue or expenditure policies, or changes in the structure of the public sector as a whole, rather than any sort of patchwork "solution" by way of additional grants to cities or increased urban access to new revenue sources.

Descending somewhat from this very general level of discussion, some particular characteristics that appear in almost all attempts to cope with problems of financing urban development may be mentioned in conclusion. One such characteristic is the striking weakness of local governments in the context of the national policy process as a whole. It is probably not too much of an exaggeration to say that municipal authorities are usually regarded by federal and provincial politicians and officials less as partners in the governmental process than as yet another interest group, and often an undesirably troublesome one. Seldom is there any degree of real negotiation between provincial and local authorities. The latter may petition; or they may object; but they almost never decide.

So long as the attitudes underlying this situation continue to prevail, there is no hope of Canadian municipalities receiving any greater control over their own fiscal destiny, nor is there any point in their doing so. If "father" (the provincial government) is convinced that "father knows best," the "children" (the municipalities) have no option but to agree, at least so long as they are small and weak. And when "father" thinks it best to *keep* them weak, there is nothing they can do about it.

Unless and until provincial governments are prepared to treat municipal authorities seriously as responsible partners, there is no reason to anticipate any deviation from recent trends to greater centralization, or provincialization, to be accurate. In a sense, many municipalities have been virtually downgraded so to speak, to field offices of the provinces — branches with troublesome delusions of autonomy, but "fortunately" without sufficient control over their own fate to mount any real opposition to the provincial governments, which are presumably omniscient and certainly omnipotent, as far as local authorities are concerned.

The provincial authorities may well, of course, be quite correct in their apparent perception of the appropriate, minimal role of relatively independent local governments. Certainly, as long as local governments are fragmented and weak, both politically and fiscally, as they now are in many areas, the expectation apparently underlying many provincial actions — that municipal actions will generally be shortsighted and inappropriate — has often had the character of a self-fulfilling prophecy. Continued emasculation of municipal autonomy may therefore result, in fact if not in name, in the conversion of all municipalities into field offices of the provincial administration, with probably no independent fiscal base other than minor fees and charges.

If local governments are to take a more constructive and active role in coping with urban problems, it is clear that they will have to be considerably strengthened to enable them to be useful partners in government rather than merely troublesome clients. A traditional argument for some degree of local autonomy in coping with local problems, for example, is the great diversity of conditions found in different localities, and the inevitable inadequacy of information about these diversities at the center. In no area is the lack of flexibility characteristic of centralized policy more of a problem than with regard to urban management. The problems of managing every city are different in detail, however similar they may be in broad outline, and in this area, as in others, it is really the details that matter in determining exactly what should be done, by whom, where, and when. Urban problems are pre-eminently local problems and must ultimately be coped with at the local level.

There is therefore a very strong case for devolving sufficient authority, including fiscal authority, to local governments organized with the sufficient territorial and functional competence to enable them to do the job. In the end, they *must* as a rule do the job anyway, whether as "independent" governments or "field offices," however hampered they may be by inadequate staff and resources and inappropriate interventions from above. It would seem better to recognize this inevitability from the beginning and to equip local governments adequately to play the role required of them. In particular, the largest cities almost certainly need different government structures, and more direct access to fiscal resources, than do other municipalities. In the interests of responsible government, however, any such increased resources should as far as possible come from local residents rather than general provincial revenues.

On the other hand, as stressed at the beginning of this chapter, the urban problem is also very much a national problem. The provincial and federal governments therefore have a legitimate, strong interest in what municipalities do, and how and when they do it. Furthermore, circumstances change from time to time in even the best-run country, so that periodic readjustments in both governmental structure and financial arrangements are needed. This need for *flexibility* to cope with changing circumstances, like the diversity of local problems and the inseparable nature of urban and national development, thus points to the need for a true partnership between all three levels of government if Canada is to cope with its urban realities. The most desirable pattern of future development therefore appears to be one of "urban partnership," or a system in which each level of government contributes both to the formulation of goals and to the determination of the appropriate instruments by which to achieve them. Only a system such as this, idealistic though it may sound to many, offers much possibility of combining local and national desires and realities in such a way as to achieve the best possible results.[1]

For municipal governments to contribute their fair share in such a system, they would perhaps have to be restructured to some extent both organizationally and in terms of finances. In particular, the larger and faster-growing urban communities may well require new forms of governmental structure, along the lines that have in fact been developed in Canada (see chapter 3). Moreover, it has been suggested in this study that the most appropriate role for local governments is to provide certain local public services efficiently (chapter 3), and the best system of finance from the point of view of both efficiency and equity is one in which local residents pay for local services either directly through user charges (chapter 6) or indirectly through a residential property or income tax (chapter 5), with broad income differentials between communities being evened out to the extent desired by provincial-municipal unconditional transfers (chapter 7).

Whether and to what extent such a restructured system would require devolving additional revenue sources to some or all urban governments should really, however, be the *outcome* of a process of negotiation and co-operative planning. It cannot, in any useful sense, be taken to be invariably the best "solution" to problems that the existing governmental structure does not yet allow to be considered in an adequately rational and comprehensive framework.

Selected Provincial-Municipal Grants in Ontario, 1979

Name of Grant	Basis of Assistance	Open-ended	Explicitly closed-ended	Implicitly closed-ended
I. Selected Unconditional grants (6 in total)				
General per capita grant	Per capita grant depends on size of population, with large municipalities receiving larger grants	–	x	–
Density per capita grant	An amount per capita varying inversely with population density	x x	–	x x
Resource equalization grant	Grant based on relative assessment deficiency of municipality and net general dollar levy	x	–	x
Special support grant	Grant provides additional percentage of net general dollar levy for municipalities in Northern Ontario plus some others	–	–	x
II. Selected Conditional nonmatching grants (11 in total)				
Municipal and County Public Library Boards	Per capita grant	–	–	x
Regional library system boards	Grant based on population and area of region plus a special grant	–	–	x
Venereal Disease Clinic	An amount per clinic attendance	–	–	x
III. Selected Conditional matching Grants (55 in total)				
15% Grants for major works	Percentage of capital cost for water supply and sewage works	–	–	x
Grants and loans to small municipalities for high-cost projects	Percentage of net project cost	–	x	–
Day nurseries — capital construction costs	Percentage of costs of new buildings computed in accordance with regulations plus percentage	–	–	x
Day nurseries — operating costs	Percentage of costs computed in accordance with regulations	–	–	x
Welfare services — administration	Percentage of cost of the administration of welfare services as defined in the regulations	–	–	x
Municipal bilingualism program	Percentage of costs	–	x	–
Homes for the aged — extended-care services	Percentage of basic rate in effect on a per diem basis plus any part of cost that exceeds ceiling	–	–	x

Name of Grant	Basis of Assistance	Open-ended	Explicitly closed-ended	Implicitly closed-ended
Community programs of recreation	Percentage of salaries of various employees plus percentage of approved maintenance and operating costs subject to a maximum	–	x	–
Ambulance services	Varying percentage of costs as approved by Minister	–	–	x
Community health facilities	Fraction of approved costs of the building project	–	–	x
Parks assistance	Varying percentage of total cost of acquisition and development to a maximum	–	x	–
Water control structures	Percentage of construction costs plus percentage of maintenance costs	–	–	x
Police radio communications services	Percentage of approved activity	–	–	x
Roads, bridges, and culverts	Percentage of construction and maintenance varying by type of municipality	–	–	x
Transportation	Percentage of subway; construction expenditures, cost of buses, trolley, transit, terminals, etc., and percentage of operating costs based on population	–	–	x
IV. *Selected unclassified conditional grants* (9 in total)				
Community planning study grants	Each application is reviewed on an individual basis			
Municipal surveys	Subject to negotiation			
Municipal housing statement grants	Each grant considered on its merits			

Source: Slack (1981).

APPENDIX B

Empirical Studies of Local Fiscal Response to Intergovernmental Transfers

The purpose of econometric studies of intergovernmental transfers is to explain statistically how grants affect expenditures. This has usually been done by using regression analysis to test the impact of grants on expenditures and, in some cases, on taxes.[1]

The impetus for the initial econometric work on the response to grants came from Fabricant (1952), who tried to explain the variation in state and local expenditures in the United States in 1942 by the variation in what are now considered to be the three "classic" independent variables: per capita income, population density, and percentage of population living in urban areas. Some years later, Fisher (1961) repeated the same experiment on a cross-sectional data base for 1957, only to discover that the explanatory power of his model was lower than that obtained by Fabricant earlier. These findings resulted in an outpouring of expenditure determinants studies. Prominent among the explanations for the decline in explanatory power was the significant increase in intergovernmental transfers that had taken place in the 15-year period between the two studies. Most subsequent studies of local expenditures have included grants as one of the independent variables assumed to affect expenditures.

These later studies, which have usually been based on cross-sectional data for state and local governments in the United States, have generally indicated that grants have a significant impact on the expenditures of the recipient government, with the magnitude of the response differing depending on the study.[2] This lack of consensus in results reflects differences in data used, in statistical techniques applied, and in the underlying theoretical model being tested. It also, of course, reflects the various possible responses of different governmental units at the different time periods analyzed.

Despite the importance of grants in Canada, few Canadian studies have been undertaken to test the impact of intergovernmental transfers on expenditures. The earlier studies were, understandably, largely modeled on the earlier U.S. studies. See, for example, Auld (1976b), Hardy (1976), Maley (1971), Michas (1969), and Rivard (1967). These studies suffered from various statistical and conceptual problems owing largely to the use of cross-sectional data and the lack of an underlying theoretical model of response.

It soon became apparent, however, that what was needed was to postulate a formal theoretical model of the expected local fiscal response to grants and then to test the model against an appropriate body of data. Two of the earliest studies based on formal models were by Henderson (1968) and Gramlich (1968). As indicated in chapter 7, these models of government behavior are based on consumer behavior models in which utility is maximized subject to a budget constraint. Governments are essentially assumed to select that amount of public expenditures and private expenditures that will maximize the utility of the community subject to a budget constraint. Henderson (1968) argued, for instance, that the utility of a community depended on community per capita personal income, community per capita revenue from federal and state governments, and population. When utility thus defined was maximized subject to a budget constraint, he ended up estimating an equation that explained per capita public expenditure as a linear function of per capita personal income, per capita grants, and population. Estimation of this equation using cross-sectional data showed *stimulation* for grants, that is, that local expenditures increased by more than the amount of the grants received.

Gramlich (1968) also maximized the utility of citizens, assuming that utility depends on public expenditures, current saving of government, and private after-tax incomes, subject to the constraint that expenditures equal revenues plus borrowing. He added some additional variables (for example, an interest-rate variable in the expenditure equation) and estimated the model using time-series data. In contrast to Henderson, Gramlich found *substitution* — grants increased expenditures by an amount less than the grant.

Subsequently, a number of other authors estimated similar models to test the response of expenditures and taxes to grants.[3] As with the earlier determinants studies, no consensus has been reached concerning the magnitude of the expenditure response to grants.

A major problem with all of the studies described thus far resulted from their failure to distinguish explicitly the price and income effects of grants on expenditures. As noted above, depending on the type of grant, there may be a price and an income effect. Most authors have neglected to consider the price effect and have estimated simple income effects models.

Several recent studies, however, have developed models that take account of the different responses to different types of transfers, including both the price and income effects.[4] The first Canadian study of this type, by Slack (1981), divides grants into unconditional grants, which are expected to alter the income of the recipient municipality, and conditional matching grants, which are expected to alter the price of the aided public service. By maximizing utility subject to a budget constraint, demand functions for local government expenditures are derived. Using pooled cross-sectional data for lower-tier municipalities in Ontario in 1973 and 1974, she estimated that unconditional grants increased local expenditures, but by an amount substantially less than the grant, and thus reduced property taxes. The results for conditional matching grants were less conclusive, however, depending on the choice of functional form. The results did show, in all cases, that the expenditure response to conditional grants exceeded the response to unconditional grants, as predicted by the theory.

Notes

2 The Institutional Setting

1. A useful overview of this history may be found in Tindal (1979), chapter 1.
2. For a description of expenditure responsibilities by province, see Canadian Tax Foundation (1981), chapter 8.
3. In 1976, for example, only about 55 percent of total government expenditure on goods and services (32 percent of total expenditure including transfers) provided "final" goods and services — primarily in the form of health care, educational and recreational services — as distinct from "intermediate" or overhead expenditures, which in themselves do not yield direct benefits to individuals. Well over half of these final consumer goods provided through the public sector were produced by local governments. For further discussion of this approach, see Bird (1979), pp. 24–25. When one takes into account also the direct impact on well-being of such generally popular local activities as streets and roads and police and fire protection — on their popularity, see Auld (1979) — the importance of the local public sector to individual well-being is obvious.
4. A brief discussion of the relative merits of alternative organizational structures for providing municipal services — departments, decentralized agencies, contracting with other suppliers (public or private) — may be found in chapter 4.
5. See Siegel (1980) for further information.
6. For a detailed discussion of provincial control of municipal planning in Ontario, see Bossons (1978), and Frankena and Scheffman (1980).
7. For a description of assessment procedures in different provinces, see Finnis (1979).
8. The same can be said of provincial governments, with more qualifications. For some discussion of the provincial role in stabilization policy, see Bird (1980b), pp. 91–117. It is generally agreed, however, that there is no local role in stabilization policy; see chapter 3.
9. Further discussion of this approach may be found in Aronson and Schwartz (1981), chapter 19.
10. An alternative way to finance capital expenditures used in some areas for new residential developments is to charge a lot levy to the developer. Such levies will usually be largely passed on in the prices of the houses. If a municipality can raise its own capital funding through lot levies in advance of providing the capital facilities, it can obviously gain some freedom from provincial constraints on budgetary decisions (see also chapter 5).

11. In 1977, for example, 73 percent of all local capital expenditures were financed out of local funds, with only Newfoundland and Prince Edward Island deviating much from this pattern (in those two provinces about two-thirds of capital expenditures were financed from grants). Particularly in urban areas, most of the local share of capital finance came from borrowing. In Manitoba in 1978, for instance, only 4 percent of city capital expenditure came from the revenue fund; in British Columbia, the comparable figure was 11 percent; in New Brunswick, 3 percent, and in Nova Scotia, 2 percent. Information from Statistics Canada and provincial reports compiled by Harry Kitchen, "Municipal Finance in Canada" (Study in preparation for Canadian Tax Foundation, 1981, chapter 5). This source also contains an extensive discussion of many other aspects of municipal capital expenditure finance in Canada. For a briefer summary, see Canadian Tax Foundation (1981), chapter 8.

12. Smaller cities with narrow industrial bases — for example, Windsor — may still, of course, face difficult problems in this respect.

13. Capital expenditures and borrowing are not included in these figures.

14. In other words, the "income elasticity" of local revenues is less than the income elasticity of expenditures. The "income elasticity of local revenues," which describes the responsiveness of local revenues to changes in income, may be calculated as the percentage change in local revenues for a given period divided by the percentage change in income over the same period. For local governments in Canada over the period 1967 to 1978, the local revenue elasticity was 0.95 for own source revenues and 1.14 for total local revenues. These figures reflect changes in both revenue bases *and* rates over this period. In other words, local own source revenues were inelastic; a one percentage increase in income resulted in a less than one percentage increase in own source revenues. Total local revenues, inclusive of transfers, however, were elastic. In comparison, the expenditure elasticity for local governments over the 1967–78 period was calculated to be 1.06, which is greater than the revenue elasticity of own source revenues but smaller than that for total revenues.

15. For an interesting development of this "restraining-rules and process" model of urban fiscal systems, see Break (1980), pp. 256–66.

3 Urban Public Economy

1. These functions coincide with the three branches of government set out in Musgrave (1959): allocation, distribution and stabilization.

2. For a detailed discussion, see Oates (1972).

3. The concept of interjurisdictional spillovers is discussed in more detail further on in this chapter.

4. In recent years, some analysts have suggested that at least the larger provinces may have some role in stabilization policy (see Bird [1980b])

but no one would reach this conclusion for even the largest cities. Similar qualifications may also be made to the Oates (1972) argument on distribution policy with respect to provincial redistribution — for example, see Breton and Scott (1978) — but again the case against *local* redistributive policies seems overwhelming.

5. For a more detailed discussion of public goods, see Musgrave and Musgrave (1980), chapters 3 and 4.

6. When the number of potential beneficiaries is small, however, a private club may be formed to provide such goods. See Buchanan (1965).

7. Note that this does not necessarily mean public production. The government may have to *provide* the good to consumers but this does not mean the government has to *produce* the good. For further discussion of the difference between public provision and public production, see chapter 4.

8. Of course, one person's enjoyment of a good may affect others when overcrowding results. In the case of a road, for example, during rush hour the road may become very congested so that each individual's use of the road affects the benefits enjoyed by others. Up to the point of congestion, however, the road can be considered to be a public good in the sense used in the text.

9. Most capitalization studies are based on American data. Among the few Canadian studies are two that indicate there is no capitalization; see Wales and Wiens (1974) on Surrey, B.C., and Chinloy (1978) on London, Ontario. A study based on Canadian data, which provides some evidence of capitalization in Toronto, however, is Hamilton (1979).

10. These words are used interchangeably throughout the text.

11. See Coase (1960).

12. See Boadway (1980, pp. 85–86) for a more detailed discussion of these issues.

13. For a more extensive discussion of these issues, see Bird and Hartle (1972).

14. For a review of various studies, see Advisory Commission (1963), and Gillespie (1971).

15. As noted earlier, other ways are by agreement between the municipalities affected, or by having an upper-level government provide subsidies to the jurisdiction generating the spillover (see chapter 7).

16. See, for example, Rothenberg (1972), and Pauly (1973).

17. For further discussion of this criterion, see Ontario Committee (1967), chapter 23.

18. These terms come from Advisory Commission (1963).

19. As noted in chapter 2, however, in Canada these laws are often provincial rather than local.

20. The information on selected cities is from Nader (1976), and Bernard, Léveillé, and Lord (1974, 1975).
21. For a summary of regional governments in Ontario, see Ontario Ministry of Treasury and Economics and Intergovernmental Affairs (1976).
22. There is little research on this matter. See, however, Cook (1973), and Ontario Ministry of Treasury and Economics and Intergovernmental Affairs (1976) for somewhat conflicting views.
23. For the most recent review of various aspects of metropolitan government in Toronto, see Robarts (1977).
24. Key works in this literature are: Downs (1957), Buchanan and Tullock (1962), Olson (1965), Niskanen (1971), Breton (1974), and Borcherding (1977). Useful summaries of these works are provided in Hartle (1976), and Mueller (1979).
25. In addition to Borcherding (1977), see especially the interesting study of Swiss municipalities by Pommerehne (1978).
26. For an extended treatment of urban public economics from this perspective, see Bish (1971).

4 Urban Expenditures

1. For further discussion of the importance of "exhaustive" expenditure and of postwar expenditure trends in general, see Bird (1979), which is the source of all the data in this section.
2. See Bird and Foot (1979) for further details.
3. See Foot (1978), p. 89.
4. See Ontario (1980), and Kitchen (in progress) for further discussion.
5. Since 1980 all education in Quebec has also been financed by provincial funds, but this is supposed to be only a provisional measure until new regional governments assume the responsibility; see Vaillancourt (1980).
6. The next three paragraphs are based largely on Bird, Bucovetsky, and Foot (1979), chapter 7.
7. These figures are taken from Kitchen, chapter 2, where their derivation and limitations are discussed at length.
8. See, for example, Ontario (1976). The following argument is based largely on Bird, Bucovetsky, and Foot (1979), chapter 5.
9. This is Festinger's theory of cognitive dissonance, as beautifully developed in Hirschman (1970). The Post Office appears to offer a telling real-world example. (Hirschman is also the source of the distinction between "exit" and "voice" discussed later in this chapter.)
10. See Aronson and Schwartz (1981), chapter 5, for a broad discussion of these and other budgeting techniques.

11. For an example with respect to police, see Scicluna, Foot, and Bird 1982.
12. A more extended discussion of this topic may be found in Bird (1980a), chapter 4.

5   Urban Revenues

1. "Grants-in-lieu" in Table 5-2 refer to payments made by other governments in lieu of property taxes. They are analytically analogous to property taxes though legally analogous to grants.
2. This is again because education is a provincial responsibility in New Brunswick. In other provinces, education grants, which are specific-purpose transfers, make up a significant portion of total grants. See also the discussion of educational finance in chapter 6.
3. See Bird and Slack (1981).
4. What scanty evidence there is suggests that businesses on average receive fewer services from local government spending than residences. Clayton (1968), for example, estimated that business got only 60 percent as much benefit. In any case, business-related services rank high among those that should be financed by user charges; see chapter 6.
5. This discussion is based largely on Bird (1976b), and Bird and Slack (1978a), chapter 3.
6. In addition, vertical space in urban areas is equivalent to "land" for many purposes. If, for example, improved building techniques permit higher buildings, the supply of "land" has in effect increased. This effect is not, of course, likely to be limited to any one jurisdiction. A different approach to the same point is taken by Grieson (1974), who argues that because the marginal cost of building a given space rises as the height of the building increases, the supply of structures is not perfectly elastic.
7. Many of these studies are summarized in Bird and Slack (1978a, Appendix A). For references to three Canadian studies, see note 9 chapter 3. All the more recent studies properly allow for the extent to which benefits accruing to property may offset taxes. Most of them also focus on the question of whether property tax *differentials* are capitalized in land values, an approach more consistent with the "new view" (further on in chapter).
8. Some shifting may, however, be accomplished through reductions in building maintenance and hence the "quality" of building services (Heilbrun 1966).
9. In addition to this limitation, traditional incidence analysis may not yield a very reliable indication of the effects on income distribution of an *existing* residential property tax for a number of reasons — the capitalization problem, the varying stages of market adjustment to past changes, and so on.

10. Although first set out by Brown (1924), and discussed by Simon (1943), this view is now usually associated with Mieszkowski (1972). Note that in this view there is no point in distinguishing between the residential and nonresidential property tax.

11. For example, in the United States property tax revenues account for 4% of the GNP compared to only 3% in Canada. The Canadian government sector is bigger, but the property tax finances a smaller part of it. This result is, of course, not surprising in view of the much more important role of provincial transfers to municipalities in Canada than in the United States. In 1970, estimated effective rates in Canadian cities ranged from around 1.8 to 3.7%, with most rates apparently in the 2–3% range (Dominion Bureau of Statistics, 1970). Some United States cities had effective rates in 1972 of 5% or more (Aaron 1975, p. 7). (United States property taxes are deductible for income tax purposes, but it is the gross incidence that is of interest here).

12. In the United States in 1972, for example, rates varied from less than 1 to over 5% (Aaron 1975, p. 7), while in Canada in 1970, the variation (in a much less comprehensive analysis) appeared to be from 1.4 to 3.7% (Dominion Bureau of Statistics, 1970).

13. This remark is based on Muller (1978), and Markusen and Scheffman (1977); the interpretation of their work in this context is entirely our own.

14. Clear evidence of the importance of intraclass variations may be found in Ontario Ministry of Treasury (1972).

15. Even in this case there are serious conceptual difficulties in analyzing the total incidence of a broad-based tax (Bird, 1980c) so that the analysis is really meaningful only when confined to tax changes — which, again, is usually the policy-relevant question in any case.

16. On present assessment biases, see Bird and Slack (1978a), pp. 13–14; also Netzer (1973).

17. See Bossons (1981) for a very critical evaluation of proposals for market-value assessment.

18. For further discussion of these factors, see Ontario Economic Council (1976).

19. See Bird and Slack (1978a) for a much fuller discussion of property tax relief measures.

20. Canadian assessing practices are described in detail in Finnis (1979). An excellent detailed introduction to property valuation for the layman is Oldman and Schoettle (1974, pp. 139–98).

21. Ontario Committee (1967), vol. 2, pp. 246–61.

22. For further discussion of the abortive property tax "reform" in Ontario, see Bird and Slack (1981).

23. See chapter 3 for a brief discussion of why it is not generally appropriate to be unduly concerned with the distributive impact of local finances.

24. On the Ontario experience, see Bird and Slack (1981).
25. This section is based on Bird and Slack (1980).
26. See Bird (1976a) chapter 11.
27. This has been particularly obvious in Ontario in the case of industrial developments, on which most municipalities have not imposed levies — though it can easily be shown that such developments may be very costly in terms of the additional facilities required to service them. There is an interesting divergence observable in municipal attitudes toward business, as opposed to residential property. As noted earlier, municipalities tend to overtax business once it is established but to undertax it in order to attract it (perhaps in part anticipating a later recoupment).
28. See studies by Levin and Hamovitch in New York (1966); for references to some Canadian studies, see Dufour and Vaillancourt (1981).
29. For an interesting discussion, see Johnson (1973).
30. For reasons similar to those discussed earlier with respect to nonresidential property taxes, local taxes on *corporate* income would be economically most ill-advised — though they would no doubt be politically most attractive.

6 Pricing Urban Services

1. See Bureau of Municipal Research (1980), p. 4. For further discussion of some of the material in the present chapter, see Bird and Slack (1980), and Bird (1976a).
2. Bird, (1976a), pp. 17–18, distinguishes quasi-private prices, public prices, fees, special assessments, and benefit taxes. For present purposes, all of these are loosely referred to here as "user charges."
3. This is another version of the benefit approach to local finance.
4. This position is, of course, really tenable in a strong form only if the upper levels of government accept that theirs is the primary redistributive responsibility.
5. See also Bird (1980a), chapter 5.
6. For an argument that the repeated attempt to redistribute through inadequate and inefficient public pricing may well have resulted in *less* overall redistribution than might otherwise have been attained, see Bird (1976a, p. 235).
7. For such a discussion, see Mushkin (1972).
8. For further discussion of this approach, see Bird (1976), chapter 4.
9. This point is developed further in Bird and Slack (1980).
10. An alternative form of rationing, by time spent in queuing rather than by money, may, of course, be considered socially preferable, as is noted in Bird (1976a), p. 41, since the poor as a rule have more time

than money. For a discussion of similar points with respect to road pricing, see Frankena (1979), chapter 4 or Frankena (1982) chapter 2.

11. Much of the following argument is based on Dennis Young (1972), chapter 4. This is really an application of the "externalities" analysis of chapter 3. See also Shenoy (1964), and Kitchen (1976).

12. This is a variant of an argument for grants; see chapter 7.

13. The power of such use of "voice" (see chapter 4) is illustrated by the frequency with which officials quote such adages as "it's the squeaking wheel that gets the grease."

14. See Downing and Gustely (1975), and Downing (1977) for citations.

15. See the review of the evidence in Downing (1973), pp. 632–33; see also Shoup (1969, pp. 141–44), for a somewhat different, though more conjectural, listing.

16. One of the most contentious issues in the creation and development of Metro Toronto hinged on this very question of whether water rates should be uniform throughout the area or not. The controversy was finally resolved in 1959 in favor of uniformity (Kaplan 1967, chapter 4). Economic rationality, it appears, often cuts little ice in the political system.

17. For a more extended appraisal of the meaning and limitations of marginal-cost pricing, see Bird (1976a), chapter 4.

18. See, for example, on Ontario, Cameron (1972), and on Nova Scotia, Nova Scotia (1974).

19. An additional source of provincial finance might be obtained by dropping the property tax credit, since much of its rationale would then have vanished — not that it has much anyway. See Bird and Slack (1978a).

20. In a sense, what is at issue here is a reversion to the original financing of education in some areas through fees or "rate bills" charged to parents (Cameron 1972).

21. For discussion see Blaug (1969), Katzman (1972), Rowley (1969), Levin (1968), Hack and Woodard (1971).

7 Provincial-Municipal Transfers

1. For a fuller list, see Slack (1981).

2. For a summary of systems in other provinces, see Ontario (1977), vol. II; see also Kwon (1979), and McMillan and Norton (1981).

3. Other ways to achieve this goal were discussed in chapter 3.

4. For a detailed analysis of alternative grant formulas, see Musgrave (1961). The "resource equalization grant" listed in Appendix A is a simple example of such a grant. The educational grant system in Ontario is an even better example; see Bird and Slack (1978b).

5. This is really the "fiscal gap" argument again.
6. See, for example, Boadway (1980), Slack (1980), and Winer (1979).
7. This analysis is based on Wilde (1968, 1971).
8. This model is derived from the standard consumer utility maximization models in economics. It is assumed that citizens of the municipality do not regard the provincial taxes that finance these grants to be a local liability.
9. Indifference curves are omitted from subsequent diagrams to simplify the presentation.
10. The following argument is made by Rasmussen (1976).
11. This assumes cost-minimization behavior.
12. For example, a capital grant for transportation purposes may result in replacement of equipment rather than increased maintenance. (Recall the discussion in chapter 4 of other incentives for government activity to be unduly capital intensive.)
13. The extent to which local governments control, for example, even property taxes is of course debatable. See chapter 2.

8   Urban Finance: A New Approach

1. For a discussion pointing in the same direction, see the paper by John Robinson in Bird (1980b). The abortive fate of the "tri-level" experience of the mid-1970s, however, does not make one very optimistic about the likelihood of future developments along these lines (see Tindal 1979, pp. 44–45).

Appendix B

1. The following summary is largely based on Bird and Slack (1978a), chapter 8 and Appendix E.
2. For a useful review, see Gramlich (1976).
3. See, for example, Struyk (1970), and Stern (1973).
4. For example, Inman (1971), Feldstein (1975), and McGuire (1978).

Bibliography

Aaron, H. 1975. *Who Pays the Property Tax?* Washington, D.C.: The Brookings Institution.

Advisory Commission on Intergovernmental Relations. 1963. *Performance of Urban Functions: Local and Areawide.* Washington, D.C.: Government Printing Office.

Amborski, David P. 1980. "Lot Levies: Service Pricing to Finance Urban Growth." Toronto, unpublished.

Aronson, J. R. and Eli Schwartz. 1981. *Management Policies in Local Government Finance.* International City Management Association.

Auld, D. A. L. 1976a. *Issues in Government Expenditure Growth.* Montreal: C. D. Howe Research Institute.

_____. 1976b. "Provincial Grants and Local Government Expenditure." *Public Finance Quarterly* 4: 295–306.

_____. 1979. "Public Sector Awareness and Preferences in Ontario." *Canadian Tax Journal* 27: 172–83.

Ballentine, J. G. and W. R. Thirsk. 1978. *The Fiscal Incidence of Some Experiments in Fiscal Federalism.* Canada Mortgage and Housing Corporation.

_____. 1980. "The Economic Consequences of Taxing Non-Residential Property." Mimeographed.

Baumol, William J. 1967. "Macroeconomics of Unbalanced Growth: The Anatomy of Urban Crisis." *American Economic Review* 57: 415–26.

Becker, A. P., ed. 1969. *Land and Building Taxes.* Madison: University of Wisconsin Press.

Bernard, A.: J. Léveillé; and G. Lord. 1974, 1975. *Profile: (Selected Cities).* Ottawa: Ministry of State for Urban Affairs.

Bird, Richard M. 1976a. *Charging for Public Services: A New Look at an Old Idea.* Toronto: Canadian Tax Foundation.

_____. 1976b. "The Incidence of the Property Tax: Old Wine in New Bottles? *Canadian Public Policy* 2, Supplement: 323–34.

_____. 1979. *Financing Canadian Government: A Quantitative Overview.* Toronto: Canadian Tax Foundation.

_____. 1980a. *Central-Local Fiscal Relations and the Provision of Urban Public Services.* Research Monograph No. 30, Centre for Research on Federal Financial Relations. Canberra: The Australian National University.

_____. ed. 1980b. *Fiscal Dimensions of Federalism*. Toronto: Canadian Tax Foundation.

_____. 1980c. "Income Redistribution Through the Fiscal System: The Limits of Knowledge." *American Economic Review, Papers and Proceedings* 90: 177-81.

Bird, R. M.; M. W. Bucovetsky; and D. K. Foot. 1978. *The Growth of Public Employment in Canada*. Toronto: Butterworths, for the Institute for Research in Public Policy.

Bird, R. M., and D. K. Foot. 1979. "Bureaucratic Growth in Canada: Myths and Realities." G. B. Doern, and A. A. Maslove, eds. *The Public Evaluation of Government Spending*. Toronto: Butterworths, for the Institute for Research in Public Policy, pp. 121–48.

Bird, Richard M., and Douglas G. Hartle. 1972. "The Design of Governments." Bird, Richard M., and John G. Head, eds. *Modern Fiscal Issues*. Toronto: University of Toronto Press.

Bird, R. M., and N. E. Slack. 1978a. *Residential Property Tax Relief in Ontario*. Toronto: University of Toronto Press, for the Ontario Economic Council.

_____. 1978b. "Property Tax Reform and Educational Finance in Ontario." Commission on Declining School Enrolment in Ontario, Working Paper 21.

_____. 1980. "Urban Finance and User Charges." Committee on Taxation, Resources and Economic Development, forthcoming.

_____. 1981. "Can Property Taxes be Reformed? — Reflections on the Ontario Experience." *Canadian Public Administration* 24: 469–85.

Bish, Robert L. 1971. *The Public Economy of Metropolitan Areas*. Chicago: Markham.

Blaug, M., ed. 1968-1969. *Economics of Education*. 2 vols. Harmondsworth, England: Penguin.

Blum, André. 1968. "Service Charges." *Municipal Finance* 41, November.

Boadway, Robin. 1979. *Public Sector Economics*. Cambridge, Mass.: Winthrop Publishers.

_____. 1980. *Intergovernmental Transfers in Canada*. Toronto: Canadian Tax Foundation.

Borcherding, Thomas E., ed. 1977. *Budgets and Bureaucrats*. Durham, N.C.: Duke University Press.

Bossons, John. 1978. *Reforming Planning in Ontario*. Toronto: Ontario Economic Council.

_____. 1981. "Property Tax Reform: What is Desirable?" Bossons, J.; M. Denny; and E. Slack, eds. *Municipal Fiscal Reform in Ontario: Property Taxes and Provincial Grants*. Toronto: Ontario Economic Council.

Bradford, D. F.; R. A. Malt; and W. E. Oates. 1969. "The Rising Cost of Local Public Services: Some Evidence and Reflections." *National Tax Journal* 22: 185-202.

Break, George F. 1980. *Financing Government in a Federal System*. Washington: Brookings Institution.

Breton, Albert. 1974. *The Economic Theory of Representative Government*. Chicago: Aldine.

Breton, Albert, and Anthony Scott. 1978. *The Economic Constitution of Federal States*. Toronto: University of Toronto Press.

Brown, H. G. 1924. *The Economics of Taxation*. New York: Henry Holt and Co.

Buchanan, James. 1965. "An Economic Theory of Clubs." *Economica* 32 (February): 1–14.

Buchanan, J., and G. Tullock. 1962. *Calculus of Consent: Logical Foundations of Constitutional Democracy*. Ann Arbor, Michigan: University of Michigan Press.

Bureau of Municipal Research. 1968. *Civic Affairs* (October).

Bureau of Municipal Research. 1970. "Market Value Reassessment" (Toronto).

Bureau of Municipal Research. 1973. "Property Taxation and Land Development." *Civic Affairs*, No. 2 (Toronto).

Bureau of Municipal Research. 1980. "Municipal Services: Who Should Pay?" Topic No. 13 (February).

Buttrick, John A. 1977. *Education Problems in Ontario and Some Policy Options*. Toronto: Ontario Economic Council.

Cameron, David M. 1972. *Schools for Ontario*. Toronto: University of Toronto Press.

Canadian Tax Foundation. 1981. *Provincial and Municipal Finances 1981*. Toronto.

Chinloy, P. 1978. "Effective Property Taxes and Property Tax Capitalization." *Canadian Journal of Economics* 11: 740–50.

Clayton, Frank. 1966. "Distribution of Urban Residential Property Tax Burdens and Expenditure Benefits in Canada." Ph.D. thesis, Queen's University.

———. 1968. "An Assessment of Proposals Affecting Property Tax Burdens." Canadian Tax Foundation. *Special Conference Report* (Toronto), pp. 47–64.

———. 1976. "Real Property Tax Assessment Practices in Canada: An Overview." *Canadian Public Policy* 2, supplement: 347–62.

Coase, Ronald. 1960. "The Problem of Social Cost." *Journal of Law and Economics* 3 (October): 1–44.

Cook, G. C. A. 1973. "Effect of Metropolitan Government on Resource Allocation: The Case of Education in Toronto." *National Tax Journal* 26: 505–90.

Crowley, R. W., and Hartwick, J. M. 1972. "Canadian Perspectives in Economics." *The Economics of Urban Growth*. Toronto: Collier-Macmillan Canada.

De Alessi, L. 1969. "Implications of Property Rights for Government Investment Choices." *American Economic Review* 59: 13–24.

Dominion Bureau of Statistics (Canada). 1970. *Principal Taxes and Rates: Federal, Provincial and Selected Municipal Governments* (Ottawa).

Downing, Paul B. 1973. "User Charges and the Development of Urban Land." *National Tax Journal* 26: 631–7.

———. ed. 1977. *Local Public Service Pricing Policies and their Effect on Urban Spatial Structure.* Vancouver, B.C.: University of British Columbia Press, for the British Columbia Institute for Economic Policy Analysis.

Downing, P. B., and R. D. Gustely. 1975. "Public Service Pricing and Urban Development: An Empirical Analysis of Fairfax County, Virginia." Center for Urban and Regional Studies, Virginia Polytechnic Institute and State University.

Downs, Anthony. 1956. *An Economic Theory of Democracy.* New York: Harper and Row.

Dufour, J.-M., and F. Vaillancourt. 1981. "Provincial and Federal Sales Taxes: Evidence of their Effect and Prospect for Change." Université de Montréal Département de Science Economique Cahier 8102.

Edel, M., and E. Sclar. 1974. "Taxes, Spending and Property Values: Supply Adjustment in a Tiebout-Oates Model." *Journal of Political Economy* 82: 941–54.

Fabricant, S. 1952. *The Trend of Government Activity in the United States Since 1900.* New York: National Bureau of Economic Research.

Feldstein, Martin S. 1974. "Incidence of a Capital Income Tax in a Growing Economy with Variable Savings Rates." *Review of Economic Studies* 4 (October): 503–513.

———. "Wealth Neutrality and Local Choice in Public Education. *American Economic Review* 65: 75–89.

Feldstein, Martin S., and Daniel Frisch. 1977. "Local Government Budgeting: The Econometric Comparisons of Political and Bureaucratic Models." Harvard Institute of Economic Research, Discussion Paper 587.

Finnis, Frederic H. 1979. *Property Assessment in Canada,* 3rd. ed. Toronto: Canadian Tax Foundation.

Fisher, G. W. 1961. "Determinants of State and Local Government Expenditures: A Preliminary Analysis." *National Tax Journal* 14: 349–55.

Fisher, R. C. 1980. "Local Sales Taxes: Tax Rate Differentials, Sales Loss, and Revenue Estimation." *Public Finance Quarterly* 8 (April): 171–87.

Flogstad, S. P. 1970. "Accounting and Financial Administration of a Swimming Pool." *Municipal Finance* 42 (May).

Foot, David K., ed. 1979. *Public Employment and Compensation in Canada: Myths and Realities.* Toronto: Butterworths, for the Institute for Research on Public Policy.

Frankena, M. W. 1979. *Urban Transportation Economics*. Toronto: Butterworths.

―――. 1982. *Urban Transportation Financing*. Toronto: University of Toronto Press, for Ontario Economic Council.

Frankena, M. W., and D. T. Scheffman. 1980. *Economic Analysis of Provincial Land Use Policies in Ontario*. Toronto: University of Toronto Press, for Ontario Economic Council.

Gillespie, W. Irwin. 1971. *The Urban Public Economy*, Urban Canada: Problems and Prospects; Research Monograph 4. Ottawa: Canadian Mortgage and Housing Corporation.

Gold, S. D. 1974. "The Distribution of Urban Government Services in Theory and Practice: The Case of Recreation in Detroit." *Public Finance Quarterly* 2 (January): 107–30.

Gramlich, Edward M. 1968. "Alternative Federal Policies for Stimulating State and Local Expenditures: A Comparison of their Effects." *National Tax Journal* 21: 119–29.

―――. 1976. "Intergovernmental Grants: A Review of the Empirical Literature." W. E. Oates, ed. *The Political Economy of Fiscal Federalism*. Lexington, Mass.: Lexington Books, 1977, pp. 219–40.

Grieson, R. E. 1974. "The Economics of Property Taxes and Land Values: The Elasticity of Supply of Structures." *Journal of Urban Economics* 1: 367–381.

Grima, Angelo. 1972. *Residential Demand for Water*. Toronto: University of Toronto, Department of Geography.

Hack, W. G., and F. Q. Woodard. 1971. *Economic Dimensions of Public School Finance*. New York: McGraw-Hill.

Hamilton, B. W. 1976. "The Effects of Property Taxes and Local Public Spending on Property Values: A Theoretical Comment." *Journal of Political Economy* 84: 647–50.

―――. 1979. "Capitalization and the Regressivity of the Property Tax: Empirical Results." *National Tax Journal*, Supplement (June): 169–80.

Hanke, S. H. 1972. "Pricing Urban Water." Selma Mushkin, ed. *Public Prices for Public Products*. Washington: The Urban Institute, pp. 283–305.

Hardy, Helen M. 1976. "Budgetary Responses of Individual Governmental Units to Federal Grants." *Public Finance Quarterly* 4: 173–86.

Hartle, D. 1976. *A Theory of the Expenditure Budgetary Process*. Toronto: University of Toronto Press, for the Ontario Economic Council.

Heilbrun, J. 1966. *Real Estate Taxes and Urban Housing*. New York: Columbia University Press.

Henderson, J. M. 1968. "Local Government Expenditures: A Social Welfare Analysis." *Review of Economics and Statistics* 50: 156–63.

Hirsch, W. Z. 1959. "Expenditure Implications of Metropolitan Growth and Consolidation." *Review of Economics and Statistics* 41.

———. 1978. "The Economics of Shirking and Its Implications for the Public Sector." H. C. Recktenwald, ed. *Secular Trends of the Public Sector.* Paris: Editions Cujas.

Hirschman, Albert O. 1970. *Exit, Voice and Loyalty.* Cambridge, Mass.: Harvard University Press.

Holland, Daniel M. 1970. *The Assessment of Land Value.* Madison: University of Wisconsin Press.

Inman, R. P. 1971. "Towards an Econometric Model of Local Budgeting." *Proceedings of the Sixty-Fourth Annual Conference on Taxation.* National Tax Association (Columbus).

Johnson, James A. 1973. "New Tax Sources and Tax-Sharing for Canadian Municipalities." *Proceedings* (Canadian Tax Foundation), pp. 591–612.

Kafoglis, Milton Z. 1969. "Local Service Charges: Theory and Practice." Harry J. Johnson, ed. *State and Local Tax Problems.* Knoxville: University of Tennessee Press.

Kaplan, Harold. 1967. *Urban Political Systems: A Functional Analysis of Metro Toronto.* New York: Columbia University Press.

Katzman, Marvin, 1972. "Pricing Primary and Secondary Education." S. Mushkin, ed. *Public Prices for Public Products.* Washington: The Urban Institute, pp. 371–93.

Kitchen, Harry M. 1975. "Some Organizational Implications of Providing an Urban Service: The Case of Water." *Canadian Public Administration* 18: 297–308.

———. 1976. "A Statistical Estimation of an Operating Cost Function for Municipal Refuse Collection." *Public Finance Quarterly:* 56–76.

———. 1977. "A Statistical Estimation of an Operating Cost Function for Municipal Water Provision." *Journal of Urban Analysis:* 119–33.

———. In progress. "Municipal Finance in Canada."

Klappholz, Kurt. 1972. "Equality of Opportunity, Fairness and Efficiency." M. Peston, and B. Corry, eds. *Essays in Honour of Lord Robbins.* London: Weidenfeld and Nicholson, pp. 246–89.

Kwon, O. Yul. 1979. "Revenue Sharing as an Improvement in Provincial-Municipal Relations in Canada: an Evaluation of Saskatchewan Revenue Sharing." *Canadian Tax Journal* 27: 576–87.

Landau, Martin. 1969. "Redundancy, Rationality and The Problem of Duplication and Overlaps." *Public Administration Review* 29: 346–58.

Levin, Henry M. 1968. "The Failure of the Public Schools and the Free Market Remedy." *The Urban Review* 2 (June): 1–15.

Maley, J. M. 1971. "The Impact of Federal Grants on Provincial Budgets: Canada." Ph.D. thesis, University of Rochester.

Markusen, J. R., and D. T. Scheffman. 1977. *Speculation and Monopoly in Urban Development: Analytical Foundations with Evidence for Toronto.* Toronto: University of Toronto Press, for the Ontario Economic Council.

McGuire, Martin. 1975. "An Econometric Model of Federal Grants and Local Fiscal Response." Oates, W. E., ed. *Financing the New Federalism*. Baltimore: Johns Hopkins, 1975.

————. 1978. "A Method for Estimating the Effect of a Subsidy on the Receiver's Resource Constraint: With an Application to U.S. Local Governments 1964–1971." *Journal of Public Economics* 10: 25–44.

McLure, C. E. 1980. "Taxes, Saving, and Welfare: Theory and Evidence," *National Tax Journal* 33: 311–20.

McMillan, M. L., and D. G. Norton. 1981. "The Distribution of Unconditional Transfers to Alberta Municipalities: Existing and Alternative Methods." *Canadian Tax Journal* 29: 171–83.

Michas, N. A. 1969. "Variations in the Level of Provincial-Municipal Expenditures in Canada: An Econometric Analysis." *Public Finance* 24: 597–613.

Mieszkowski, P. 1972. "The Property Tax: An Excise Tax or a Profits Tax?" *Journal of Public Economics* 1: 73–96.

Mueller, D. C. 1979. *Public Choice*. Cambridge: Cambridge University Press.

Muller, R. A. 1978. *The Market for New Housing in the Metropolitan Toonto Area*. Toronto: Ontario Economic Council.

Musgrave, Richard. 1959. *The Theory of Public Finance*. New York: McGraw-Hill.

————. 1961. "Approaches to a Fiscal Theory of Political Federalism." National Bureau of Economics Research. *Public Finances: Needs, Sources and Utilization*. Princeton: Princeton University Press.

————. 1974. "Is a Property Tax on Housing Regressive?" *American Economic Review*, Papers and Proceedings, 64 (May): 222–29.

Musgrave, Richard, and Peggy B. Musgrave. 1980. *Public Finance in Theory and Practice*, 3rd ed. New York: McGraw-Hill.

Mushkin, Selma, ed. 1972. *Public Prices for Public Products*. Washington: The Urban Institute.

Nader, George. 1976. *Cities of Canada, Volume Two: Profiles of Fifteen Metropolitan Centres*. Toronto: MacMillan.

Netzer, D. 1973. "The Incidence of the Property Tax Revisited." *National Tax Journal* 26 (December): 515–36.

New York University. 1966. *Financing Government in New York City*. Final Research Report of the Graduate School of Public Administration to the Temporary Commission on City Finances.

Niskanen, W. A. 1971. *Bureaucracy and Representative Government*. Chicago: Aldine-Atherton.

Nova Scotia. 1974. *Report of the Royal Commission on Education, Public Services and Provincial-Municipal Relations* (Halifax).

Oates, Wallace E. 1972. *Fiscal Federalism*. New York: Harcourt Brace Jovanovich.

Oldman, O., and F. P. Schoettle. 1974. *State and Local Taxes and Finance*. Mineola, N.Y.: The Foundation Press.

Olson, Mancur, Jr. 1965. *The Logic of Collective Action: Public Goods and the Theory of Groups*. Cambridge, Mass.: Harvard University Press.

Ontario. 1977. *Report of the Provincial-Municipal Grants Reform Committee*, 2 vols. (Toronto).

Ontario. 1980. *Local Government Finance in 1977 and 1978* (Toronto).

Ontario Committee on Taxation. 1967. *Report*, 3 vols. Toronto: Queen's Printer.

Ontario Economic Council. 1976. *Issues and Alternatives — Housing* (Toronto).

Ontario Ministry of Treasury and Economics and Intergovernmental Affairs. 1972. *Analysis of Income and Property Taxes in Guelph* (Toronto).

_____. 1976. *Regional Government in Perspective: A Financial Review*, Ontario Tax Studies 11 (Toronto).

Orzechowski, W. P. 1974. "Labour Intensity, Productivity, and the Growth of the Federal Sector." *Public Choice* 19: 123–26.

Pauly, M. V. 1973. "Income Redistribution as a Local Public Good." *Journal of Public Economics* 2.

Peterson, G. 1972. "The Regressivity of the Residential Property Tax." Working Paper No. 1207–10, The Urban Institute, Washington, D.C.

Polinsky, A. M., and D. L. Rubinfeld. 1974. "The Long-Run Incidence of a Residential Property Tax and Local Public Services." Working Paper No. 1207–29, The Urban Institute, Washington, D.C. (February).

Pommerehne, Werner, W. 1978. "Institutional Approaches to Public Expenditures: Empirical Evidence from Swiss Municipalities." *Journal of Public Economics* 9: 255–80.

Rasmussen, Jon. 1976. "The Allocative Effects of Grants-in Aid: Some Extensions and Qualifications." *National Tax Journal* 29: 211–19.

Rivard, Jean-Yves. 1967. "Determinants of City Expenditures in Canada." Ph.D. thesis, University of Michigan.

Robarts, John. 1977. *Report of the Royal Commission on Metropolitan Toronto*, 2 vols. (Toronto).

Robinson, A. J. 1971. *Economic Evaluation of Municipal Expenditures: PPB*. Toronto: Canadian Tax Foundation.

Rothenberg, J. 1972. "Local Decentralization and the Theory of Optimal Government." Edel, M., and Rothenberg, J., eds. *Readings in Urban Economics*. New York: The MacMillan Company.

Rowley, C. K. 1969. "The Political Economy of British Education." *Scottish Journal of Political Economy* 16: 152–76.

Schultze, C. L. 1974. "Sorting out the Social Grant Programs: An Economist's Criteria." *American Economic Review* 64: 181–89.

Scicluna, E.; D. Foot; and R. Bird. 1982. "Productivity in the Public Sector:

The Case of Police Services." Robert H. Haveman, ed. *Public Finances and Public Employment: Proceedings of the 36th Congress of the International Institute of Public Finance, Jerusalem, 1980.* Detroit: Wayne State University Press.

Seldon, Arthur. 1977. *Change.* London: Temple Smith.

Shenoy, S. 1967. "Pricing for Refuse Removal." Institute of Economic Affairs. *Essays in the Theory and Practice of Pricing* (London).

Shoup, Carl. 1969. *Public Finance.* Chicago: Aldine Publishing Co.

Siegel, D. 1980. "Provincial-Municipal Relations: An Overview." *Canadian Public Administration* 23: 281-317.

Simon, H. A. 1943. "The Incidence of a Tax on Urban Real Property." R. A. Musgrave, and C. S. Shoup, eds. *Readings in the Economics of Taxation.* Homewood, Illinois: Richard D. Irwin, 1959.

Slack, Enid. 1980. "Local Fiscal Response to Intergovernmental Transfers." *Review of Economics and Statistics* 62: 364-70.

———. 1981. "Provincial-Municipal Grant Reform in Ontario" in Bossons, J., M. Denny and E. Slack, *Municipal Fiscal Reform in Ontario: Property Taxes and Provincial Grants* (Ontario Economic Council).

Statistics Canada. *Local Government Finance* (annual).

Statistics Canada. *National Income and Expenditure Accounts* (quarterly).

Statistics Canada. (1980), *Perspectives Canada III.*

Stern, D. 1973. "Effects of Alternative State Aid Formulas on the Distribution of Public School Expenditures in Massachusetts", *Review of Economics and Statistics,* 55, 91-7.

Struyk, Raymond J. 1970. "Effects of State Grants-in-Aid on Local Provision of Education and Welfare Services in New Jersey", *Journal of Regional Science,* 10, 225-35.

Stubblebine, W. C. 1965. "Institutional Elements in the Financing of Education", *Southern Economic Journal* 32.

Thompson, Wilbur. 1969. "The City as a Distorted Price System", *Psychology Today* 2, 30-3.

Tiebout, Charles M. 1956. "A Pure Theory of Local Government Expenditures", *Journal of Political Economy,* 64, 416-24.

Tindal, C. R. and S. N. Tindal. 1979. *Local Government in Canada* (Toronto: McGraw-Hill Ryerson).

Vaillancourt, Francois. 1980. "Financing Local Authorities in Quebec — The Reform of Bill 57" *Canadian Tax Journal,* 28 (May-June), 274-88.

Vickrey, William S. 1963. "General and Specific Financing of Urban Services," in Howard G. Schaller (ed.) *Public Expenditure Decisions in the Urban Community* 62-90 (Baltimore: The Johns Hopkins Press for Resources for the Future Inc.).

Wales, T. J. and F. G. Wiens. 1974. "Capitalization of Residential Property

Taxes: An Empirical Study", *Review of Economics and Statistics*, 56, 329–333.

Wilde, James A. 1968. "The Expenditure Effects of Grants-in-Aid Programs", *National Tax Journal*, 21, 340–8.

_____. 1971. "Grants-in-Aid: The Analytics of Design and Response", *National Tax Journal*, 24, 143–55.

Winer, Stanley L. 1979. "Some Evidence on the Effect of the Separation of Spending and Taxing Decisions", Discussion Paper, Carleton University.

Young, Dennis. 1972. *How Shall We Collect the Garbage?* (Washington: The Urban Institute).

Index